HOW TO TEACH
BEGINNING
BALLET

HOW TO TEACH BEGINNING BALLET

The First Three Years

Judith Newman

Princeton Book Company, Publishers

Princeton Book Company, Publishers
614 Route 130
Hightstown, NJ 08520

Cover design by High Tide Design
Book design by E. Helmetsie
Student photographs by Shelley Gefter

Printed in the United States of America

Publisher's Cataloging-In-Publication Data
Newman, Judith, 1942-
　　How to teach beginning ballet : the first three years / Judith Newman.
　　　　p. : ill. ; cm.

　　ISBN: 978-0-87127-374-1
　　1. Ballet--Study and teaching (Elementary) 2. Ballet dancing--Handbooks, manuals, etc. 3. Dance for children--Study and teaching (Elementary) I. Title. II. Title: Ballet

GV1788.5 .N485 2012
372.86/8

Contents

3   IN THE CENTER

4   TRANSITION STEPS

5   PETITE ALLEGRO

6   THE END OF CLASS

Part II

1   AT THE BARRE

Part IV

Introduction

WHY A HOW-TO BOOK

Like many professional dancers, I never gave much thought to what I would do when my career came to an end. I certainly never planned to be a ballet teacher. But then I met my husband, also a dancer, and off we went to have a "real life." Our plan was to find a means of support while my husband went back to school to earn a degree in business. Suddenly, teaching seemed like a good idea.

Coincidently, my mother-in-law was a ballet teacher, and because she was about to retire, she graciously recommended us to her students. We rented a hall, bought a record player and a few records (the year was 1970!), put an ad in the paper, and opened for business. That was the easy part. The hard part was facing my first class of seven year-olds. I didn't have a clue. Sure, I was a professional ballet dancer, but I hadn't given much thought to how I became one. I knew how to put a class together and make up combinations, but I had never thought about what someone who had never danced before needed to learn.

I decided to ask my first ballet teacher, Thomas Armour, for advice, and to my delight, he sent me a syllabus he had created some time ago, the same one that had guided my early training. The syllabus was invaluable. It laid out for me the steps appropriate to every level of training. But as I began to teach I realized there was still so much I didn't know. I had "the what," not "the how." I had never explored what skills were needed to execute a simple step. I had never tried to explain what a movement felt like. I had never learned the physics of movement, how to coax out a feeling, how to fix someone else's problems, handle an attitude, command attention, motivate, inspire trust. I searched through many wonderful books, and while I discovered a great deal of information on the history of dance, anatomy, vocabulary, early childhood education, and creative dance, there was little advice about teaching ballet to beginning students. Ultimately, I had to figure out the process myself.

Over the next thirty years, whenever I shared my early experiences with other teachers, I found that we all seemed to have started out much the same way, learning on the job by trial and error. For that reason, I decided to write this book, a survival guide, so to speak, for the novice teacher.

I have chosen to focus on the first three years of the syllabus, the elementary levels, designed for children who are seven years of age or older and ready, both physically and mentally, to train seriously. Of the ten years it takes to produce a dancer, I believe the first three years are the most important. During that time, every skill needed to dance is learned and practiced, habits both good and bad are formed, pathways between brain and body are laid out, and quality is defined and demonstrated. Everything that follows rests on the foundation of the first three years.

In the text, I have included the syllabus that served me so well during my career, a plan for moving through the syllabus, and a discussion of how those steps listed in the syllabus should be executed both physically and aesthetically. Throughout, I suggest ways to teach effectively and offer solutions to problems that may arise.

As you enter the classroom for the first time, as you take on the responsibility of passing on the grand tradition of classical ballet, it is my hope that this book will support and inspire you and that your efforts will bring you the fulfillment that only this profession can bring.

PREPARING TO TEACH

If I were to ask you what kind of teacher you would like to be, you would probably say knowledgeable, energetic, fair, inspiring, caring, able to leap tall buildings, etc, and though I would not dissuade you from being all those things, I would suggest that as you start out, no matter what kind of teacher you would like to be, you should be one that is prepared.

Being prepared usually refers to the composition of class material, but it encompasses so much more. It means you have thought about your students since you last taught them, remembered who needs to be reminded of a correction or who needs a word of encouragement. It means you know if your car has enough gas to get to the studio. It means that you have allowed yourself time to warm-up before class. It means that you have cleared your mind of distractions so that you can be present to your students the moment they enter the classroom.

Preparing for a new job

If you are a new teacher and have been hired as a substitute or a full time teacher, being prepared will not only inspire confidence in your students and your employer, it will lessen the anxiety that comes when facing the unknown. Before you teach, ask questions about anything that might ease your way into the classroom.

1. Where is the studio and when does the class begin?
2. How much will I be paid?
3. How old are the students, how long have they studied, and how many classes do they take a week?
4. What skills/steps/combinations are they working on at the barre and in the center?
5. How long is the class?
6. How many students are in the class?
7. What kind of floor does the studio have?
8. What are the rules of conduct and dress?
9. Will I be required to take the roll?
10. What musical accompaniment or equipment is available?

Visit the school, if possible, and observe the class or classes you will be teaching. See for yourself!

Preparing class material

Based on the information you gather, begin to compose your class. If you have observed the class you are about to teach, use the class structure and material of the teacher you are replacing so that the students have continuity. Even if you are taking over a class on a full time basis, model the class of the previous teacher for a short time. Introduce changes slowly, mindful of the comfort of your students.

To make sure your combinations are musical, hum a familiar tune or recite a nursery rhyme as you compose them. The duple-meter of Little Bo Peep and Jingle Bells provides excellent accompaniment for battement tendu and grand battement while the triple-meter of Home on the Range, Silent Night, and Lullaby and Goodnight aptly supports grand plié and rond de jambe à terre. Better yet, purchase your own CD. That way you can test the musicality of your combinations before class and know in advance which tracks you need to use during class.

Compose a class that contains too much material rather than too little. If time runs out, better to leave out a combination than be caught short with nothing to do.

Memorize your class. Students will become rowdy and muscles will get cold if you spend time shuffling through your notes.

IN THE CLASSROOM

When you enter the classroom for the first time, you may not feel like a seasoned teacher, but there are ways to appear like one.

1. *Dress the part*

   Don't model yourself after professional dancers who often look like raga-muffins when they take class or rehearse. Just as you need to see the line and placement of your students, so they need to learn from and be inspired by your example. Don't cover up your neck, arms, mid-section, legs, or feet. Smell good!

2. *Speak loud and clear*

   This seems so simple, but it is hard to control your voice when you are nervous. Practice demonstrating your combinations vocally. Project your voice to the farthest wall much like a dancer projects movement to the back of a theatre. Let it demonstrate the energy, the accents, the rhythms, and the movement quality of a combination.

   Use French terminology to describe the movements of a combination. Say "battement tendu quatrième devant" instead of "point front." Practice your pronunciation and know the meaning of the words. Invest in a good ballet dictionary. I highly recommend The Language of Ballet by Thalia Mara (published by Dance Horizons).

3. *Move about*

   Nerves make it especially difficult to walk and talk at the same time. It feels much easier and safer to stand in one place and hold onto something while you teach. Roaming about the classroom, however, gives your students at least the impression that you are interested in seeing everyone and everything even if you are too self-conscious in the beginning to notice much. The students need to feel your eyes on them. Later, as your confidence increases, observing the dancers from different angles allows you to correct mistakes that you could never see standing or sitting in one place.

4. *Demonstrate correctly and beautifully*

   Young children learn to dance in the beginning primarily by mimicking. Since you are the one they will mimic, it is important that you demonstrate correctly and beautifully. If you sickle your foot, chances are so will your students. If you do not use your head, hands, and upper body expressively, neither will they. If your voice is flat, their dancing will be, too. Show them how you want it done. Perform it! Marking does not mean to shuffle through a combination. You don't have to jump or turn, but line, shape, direction, and expression should be clear.

   Face the mirror when demonstrating. That way the right leg of the teacher is on the right side of the student. Facing the mirror also allows you to see the whole class. When you face the class, it feels as if the students are on top of you.

5. *Manage your time*

Be early. Give yourself time to warm-up your body and to review your class material and the specific goals you want to achieve that day. Rushing causes stress, and stress will affect the quality of your teaching.

Start on time. Students learn punctuality by example. If you start your class late, your students will begin to arrive even later. Punctuality means you are disciplined and serious about your work.

Keep track of time. Students certainly need information and attention, but not at the expense of a well-balanced, evenly-paced class. Sometimes it is necessary to be quiet and just let the dancers dance.

Finish on time. Respect the teacher and the class that follow.

Repeat a class two or three times if you feel you are not getting the job done in one class period. This will help your students learn the material thoroughly. It will also give them a sense of mastery and a respect for the rehearsal process.

6. *Learn the names of your students*

If you teach a group of students more than one time, learn everyone's name by the second class. This is an important step in developing a bond with a child. Every dancer knows the joy of hearing her name called out in class.

The importance of remembering names was brought home to me during my first year of teaching. I noticed that a student had been absent since the first class of the term. I spoke to her mother, and she explained that her daughter had come home crying that first day. When I asked why, she said it was because I never called her by her name. I apologized, but the little girl never wanted to come back. I lost a student but learned a valuable lesson about the sensitivity of children.

STARTING FROM SCRATCH

If you open your own studio or are hired full-time to teach for someone else, hopefully you will have the opportunity to work with a group of beginning students over an extended period of time. This is the most satisfying teaching experience because it allows you to observe the effectiveness of your work. It is also the most challenging because it is left to you to determine how to proceed. The challenge may seem daunting until you begin to discover the wonderful logic that orders ballet technique.

The first class

Use the first few classes to gently ease your new students into the world of dance. Answer their questions, calm their fears, be a real person, excited to teach them what you know and love.

1. Begin the class with a quiet time to allow the students to settle down and focus. Sit on the floor in a circle. Tell the class your name and a little about yourself and ask the students to do the same. See if you can match a name to each face by the end of class.

2. Give the students a tour of the studio.

3. Explain the purpose of the mirror and the barre.

4. Explain why the class is divided into barre work and center work.

5. Show them how to tie and tuck in the strings of their ballet shoes.

6. Show them how to stand in staggered lines so they can see themselves in the mirror as they work in the center. Teach them how to change lines so that all students have a turn to stand in front.

7. Demonstrate the five positions of the feet, standing in front of the mirror, hands on hips. Explain that all the steps in ballet either begin or end in one of these positions. Ask the students to follow you as you show each one again. Don't bother with form for the moment. Just let the class enjoy using their legs in strange and new ways.

8. Practice flexing and pointing the feet, sitting on the floor in a circle, shoes off (see page 21). Use your hands to help the students achieve the desired shape.

9. Discuss how to stand and hold the barre correctly (see page 23).

10. Show the class how to create the shape of first position by standing with the feet parallel and opening the feet to shape a letter V (see page 24). Invite the class to try.

11. Introduce a demi-plié in first position (see page 26). Pronounce the name of the step, explain its meaning, spell it on a chalkboard, and have the students repeat it after you. Explain that all the names of the steps are in French because ballet first began in that country a long time ago, about the time the Pilgrims came to America. Continue to quiz them on the meaning and pronunciation of the demi-plié throughout the class.

12. Ask if someone would like to try this step. Work with the volunteer at the barre. Review how to stand properly. Explain to the class that you will be correcting each student often because part of your job is to help them improve. Ask if anyone else would like to try the demi-plié. Continue until everyone has a turn.

13. Place the students in staggered lines. Ask them to make an oval or egg shape with their arms, a position called low fifth (see page 20).

14. Introduce the positions of the head (see page 13). Sit cross-legged on the floor and demonstrate how the head moves on top of the neck. Incline the head right and left, turn the head right and left, and lift the chin up and down.

15. Play the game of "mud puddle." Place an object like a towel in the center of the room and designate the object as the "mud puddle." Line students up in the corner and ask them to run and jump over it.

16. Ask them questions about what they have learned so far.

17. Move to music. Ask the students to follow you as you move your body and arms through space. Pay no attention to form, but let them experience the pleasure of responding physically to rhythm and melody. Teach them the meaning of a révérance and how it is used to thank the teacher at the end of class.

18. Remember to prepare more material than you think you will need. Having too much is better than having too little.

The second class

1. Sit in a circle and play the name game. Get them all right! Check on attire. Acknowledge those students who are dressed correctly. Give students time to adjust to the rules, but set a deadline and communicate what consequences will be given if those rules are broken. Explain why it is important to be on time, to dress properly, and to pay attention.

2. Quiz the children. Ask them questions about everything they learned in the last class.

3. Review the five positions of the feet. Invite the students to follow you as you demonstrate each one. Show the positions out of order and ask the class to name them.

4. Practice flexing and rolling through the feet. Sit on the floor in a circle without shoes. Let the students correct you and each other. Ask the class why dancers need corrections.

5. Review the head positions. Practice by sitting on the floor facing the mirror. Move from one position to another with music.

6. Review the demi-plié. Ask what the word means. Ask who can spell it. Ask someone to explain how to do it correctly. Execute the step incorrectly and ask the students to "fix" you.

7. Make the shape of an oval (low fifth) with the arms. Add a new shape, a circle (middle fifth).

8. Play jump over the mud-puddle moving downstage on a diagonal (corner to corner).

9. Listen to music and ask students to describe the quality of the sound. Is it strong or soft, smooth or sharp, does it remind them of some action or feeling? Clap and count.

10. To end the class, ask the students to follow you in a freeform movement sequence.

The third class and beyond—presenting new material

1. Review any new material learned in the previous class by asking the students to show or tell you what they remember. Give high praise to those students who remember information or a correction. Re-teach only if everyone has forgotten the material.

2. Before introducing a new step, work backwards to determine the set of skills needed to perform the new step. Practice the skills first and when they have been mastered, teach the step.

   Consider, for example, the demi-plié. Because the step is performed standing, the student must be aware of correct posture. Because it is performed at the barre, she must know how to hold the barre. Because it is executed from first position with the arm held in low fifth, she must know how to shape these positions. All these skills must be in place before the step can be attempted.

   Think about the composition of a battement tendu à la seconde, how a dancer must know how to stretch and turn out the leg, how to move through the foot from one position to another, how to point the foot, and where to direct the leg.

   After a while, you will find there are no new skills left to teach, only new steps.

3. When introducing a new step, show it, name it, spell it on the chalkboard, and define it. First break the step down and practice each part separately. Next, put all the parts together. Break down and reassemble a step as often as necessary.

4. Correct patiently. Praise when warranted. Work with each student individually. Allow the students to teach each other.

5. As soon as a step is mastered at the barre, move it to the center.

6. As soon as one step is mastered, introduce a new one.

7. When two steps have been mastered, combine them and add music.

8. Move from the easy to the difficult. For example, extending the leg or moving to the side is easier than extending or moving to the front. Extending the leg or moving to the front is easier than extending or moving to the back. Lifting the leg from pointe tendue is easier than extending it from the ankle. An elevé is easier than a relevé.

In the early months of training, you will be moving from the floor, to the barre, to the center, back to the floor, to a chair, or anywhere your material takes you, but as soon as the students know how to stand and hold the barre, shape first position of the feet, execute a demi-plié, position the arm in low and middle fifth, and extend the leg à la second and quatrième devant, enough material will be available for a rudimentary barre. Once that barre is combined with a center consisting of gentle floor stretches, port de bras, a musical game, and movement across the floor, you have the semblance of a class.

As the class increases in complexity, use the following guidelines to make sure it is balanced both physically and mentally.

1. Alternate slow exercises with quick exercises.

2. Let extensions progress gradually from low to high.

3. Alternate the simple with the complex.

4. Repeat to strengthen but not to exhaust.

Part I

Elementary 1: Syllabus for the First Year

As you move through the lessons below, keep in mind that it is a guideline, not a timetable. Each group of students will have its own personality, its own rhythm and energy. One class might excel in some areas but be weak in others. One year you might have a group that moves into second year work at the beginning of the summer while another might need to repeat material from the first year well into the second year. Let the syllabus point the way, but, at the same time, adapt the syllabus to the needs of your students.

Preparatory exercises:
Positions of the head
Positions of the feet
Positions of the arms

Barre exercises:
Demi-plié in positions one, two, and five
Grand plié in positions one and two
Battement tendu à la seconde, quatrième devant, and quatrième derrière
Battement tendu relevé à la seconde
Battement tendu à la seconde, flexing and pointing
Battement soutenu simple à la seconde
Dégagé en l'air à la seconde
Rond de jambe à terre in four counts
Battement frappé à la seconde, single in two counts and double in four counts
Elevé and relevé in first position
Soussus
Attitude à la seconde
Sur le cou-de-pied devant and derrière
Battement retiré devant
Grand battement à la seconde in four counts

Center exercises:
Floor stretches
First, second, and third, arabesque
Glissade derrière and devant
Sauté in first position
Changement de pieds
Échappé sauté
Assemblé dessus

Soubresaut

Sissonne fermé de côté dessus

Chassé

Grand jeté

Triplets

Pony steps

Chaînés turns

Révérance

Note that sidebars are used throughout the book to emphasize a point or delve more deeply into a subject.

As you move through the text, note that each step is discussed according to the way in which it builds on the previous step and/or prepares for the following step. The sample combinations included in the various sections are meant to suggest ways in which new material can be presented.

The meter of the appropriate musical accompaniment is given at the start of each sample combination. The meter indicates the way in which time has been divided, duple-meter, 2/4 or 4/4, and triple-meter, 3/4 or 6/8. Each movement of a combination is assigned a count or a smaller division of that count called a pulse that comes before or after a count. For example, a four-count grand plié accompanied by a triple-meter is written as follows: demi-plié (1-&-a)/grand plié (2-&-a)/demi-plié (3-&-a)/straighten (4-&-a). Accompanied by a duple-meter, three single frappés and one double frappé beginning from pointe tendue à la seconde are written like this: single (&-1)/single (&-2)/single (&-3)/double (&-a-4).

BEFORE THE BARRE  1

Positions of the head

During the first year, students normally work with the head erect. In this position, the back of the neck continues the line of the spine, the line of the chin runs parallel to the floor, and the eyes focus toward the horizon. Some basic head positions, however, should be introduced so that the students learn how to move the head on top of the neck without affecting any other part of the body, a skill that is the foundation of artistic expression.

To better feel how the torso is affected when the head changes positions, sit cross-legged on the floor with the hands on the knees. Incline the head to the right and to the left, turn the head to the right and to the left, raise the head, and lower the head. Whichever way the head moves, keep the spine elongated and the shoulders level. Whenever the head is lowered, maintain a space between the chin and the chest.

When the students are able to execute each position correctly, link them together, transitioning from one to the other through the erect position. Perform with music when the class is ready. The combination below, or one like it, is a good way to focus the attention of the students at the start of the class.

> Use a triple-meter. Tilt the head to the right (1-&-a)/return to center (bring the head erect) (2-&-a)/tilt the head to the left (3-&-a)/return to center (4-&-a)/turn the head right (5-&-a)/ return to center (6-&-a)/turn the head left (7-&-a)/return to center (8-&-a)/lift the chin up (1-&-a)/return to center (2-&-a)/lower the chin toward the chest (3-&-a)/return to center (4-&-a)/rest four counts (5-8). Repeat.

Inclined

Turned

Raised

Positions of the feet

Introduce all the positions of the feet in the center, facing the mirror so that the students are able to follow as you demonstrate. Note that students will need to walk the working foot from one position to another until they learn how to execute a battement tendu and a demi-rond de jambe a terre.

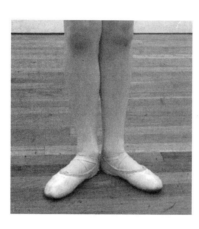

First position

Form a letter V, placing the toes equidistant from a center line that runs perpendicular to the body and dissects the shape.

Second position

Place the heels just outside of the shoulders, feet at equal angles.

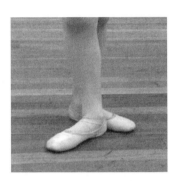

Third position

Place the heel of the front foot at the middle of the back foot, feet at equal angles.

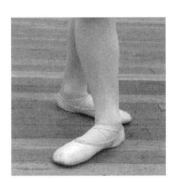

Fourth position

From third position, move the front foot forward a distance equivalent to the length of the student's foot. Wait until the introduction of a grand pliè in fourth position to line up the toes precisely with the heels.

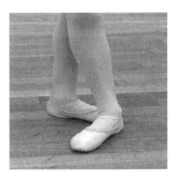

Fifth position

Place the heel of the front foot in front of the toes of the back foot and, with the feet at equal angles, shape a V that faces to the side. The distance between the heel of the front foot and the toes of the back foot will depend on the size of the upper leg

Positions of the arms

The French, Cecchetti, and Russian schools assign different numbers to the same arm positions. A standardized version, commonly used in the U.S., takes from all three schools and consists of five basic positions, demi-seconde, and four variations of the basic five, including low third, high third, low fifth, and middle fifth.

Once the students have learned the five basic positions of the arms, combine them with the positions of the feet. Teach the remaining positions as they are needed. Because each arm position is some combination of a circle, an oval, or half of a circle or an oval, know that the students will be able to shape any position correctly as soon as they know how to make those shapes.

First
Open the shape of an oval, placing the fingertips next to the thighs.

Second
Extend both arms from the shoulders to the sides of the body. Draw half of an oval, a small letter C, with each arm. Draw a big letter C from the fingertips of one hand to the fingertips of the other hand.

Middle third

Extend one half of the oval (a small letter C) from one shoulder to the side of the body and draw a half circle with the other arm, placing it in front of the body, fingertips at mid-line, hand lower than the elbow.

Fourth position

Starting from middle third, keep the half circle in front of the body and bring the oval, extended to the side of the body, overhead.

High fifth

Shape an oval over the head. Be able to see the palms of the hands while keeping the head still and looking up with the eyes only.

Demi-seconde

Shape an upside down cereal bowl with both arms.

Low third

Extend one arm from the shoulder to the side of the body, drawing half an oval. Place the other half of the oval in front of, but without touching the thigh.

High third

Extend one half of the oval from the shoulder to the side of the body and place the other half (a letter C) overhead.

Low fifth

Shape an oval with both arms, placing the hands in front of, but without touching the thighs.

Middle fifth

Round both arms in front of the body, placing the fingertips between the chest and the waist.

Pointing the foot

Pointing the foot tapers the line of the leg, making it beautiful to look at.

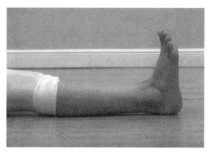

Flexed

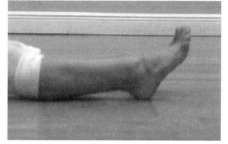

Demi-pointe

Sit on the floor with one leg extended in front of the body, knee straight and foot flexed. Push through the ball of the foot until the top of the ankle is stretched (demi-pointe) and then lengthen the toes. To return to the starting position, bend the toes, keeping the knee and the top of the ankle stretched (demi-pointe) and then flex the foot. Repeat this exercise carefully and often to prepare for battement tendu à la seconde, demi-pointe, and jumping.

When pointing the foot, think of elongating the entire leg. Keep the hips square and try to touch the opposite wall with the tips of the first three toes. The energy that runs through the leg to point the foot is the same energy that will one day be used to support the body en pointe.

Incorrect

Incorrect

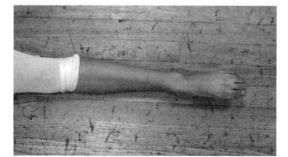

Correct

Looking at the leg from above, make sure that the ankle continues the line of the leg. It should not curve in (sickle) or curve out (bevel). Catch these problems early. Once they become habitual, they are difficult to correct and may lead to injuries over time. Shape your feet properly as well. Don't forget that your students model you.

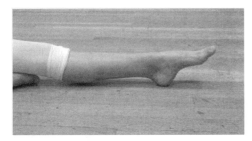

Incorrect

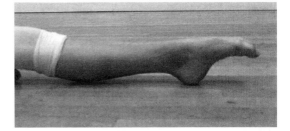

Incorrect

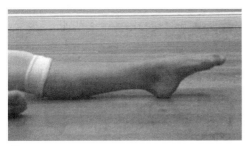

Correct

Explore how the actions of the toes affect the leg. First, curl the toes under, then relax the toes, and finally stretch the toes. Notice how curling or gripping causes the calf to contract, shortening the leg. Pretend that the hand is a foot. Reach toward a wall and then make a fist. The arm will feel light and long when the hand reaches, heavy and short when the hand makes a fist.

With regard to the line of the leg, remember that a stretched knee is as important as a well-shaped foot. If a student has difficulty keeping the knee stretched as the foot points, encourage her to practice the exercise slowly until she is able to make a connection between the two actions. Like a beveled or sickled foot, this problem is difficult to correct once it becomes a habit.

2 AT THE BARRE

Hand on the barre

I prefer that beginning students work with one hand on the barre as soon as possible. Other teachers feel strongly that students should work with both hands

on the barre for a full year. Both have advantages and disadvantages. Whatever you decide, always be aware of how your students are holding the barre. Are they gripping, leaning on, or pulling away from it? Are they using the barre instead of their legs to balance?

When placing one hand on the barre, rest it slightly in front of the shoulder, as if in second position. Keep this position fixed except when the body shifts forward to allow the leg to extend to the back. When this occurs, slide the hand forward so that the hand/shoulder relationship is maintained. When both hands are placed on the barre, keep them shoulder-width apart, allowing them to slide along the barre whenever the weight shifts from side to side.

Turn-out

In France, during the seventeenth century, a new art form emerged called the opera-ballet, a grand entertainment combining the dances of the court with music and song, all for the purpose of telling a story. Presented in a stage-like setting before an audience, dancers who performed in these productions found it necessary to move from side to side or on a diagonal so that they could be seen by everyone. They began turning out their legs to make it easier to move in these directions. Over time, turn-out became the foundation of ballet technique and came to define the aesthetics of the art form.

Moving through the text, how turn-out works and how it applies to the elementary repertoire, will be discussed in detail. Meanwhile, it is necessary to understand the rules that guide this action.

1. Turn-out is achieved by rotating the legs in the hip socket.
2. Turn-out is possible only when there is resistance to it.
3. The degree of turn-out increases or decreases depending on the proximity of one leg to another, if the knees are bent or straight, or if one foot is flat or pointed, à terre or en l'air, front, side, or back.
4. Turn-out is stressful to the body and must be cultivated gradually and with care.

First position

As a prelude to first position, discuss why and how dancers turn-out their legs. Practice the position lying on the floor. Hold the legs parallel in the air with the feet flexed and rotate both legs at the same time to open the feet. With no weight to support, the students will be able to feel how the legs, moving in the hip sockets, dictate the placement of the knees and the feet.

At the barre, stand with the feet parallel, one hand on the barre and the other hand at the waist. Keeping the heels together, open the toes of both feet simultaneously to form a V-shape. This method of shaping first position insures that both legs rotate simultaneously from the hips to place the toes of both feet equidistant from the center line.

As the students practice, make sure they feel rather than look at what is happening below the waist.

Posture

As soon as the class knows how to hold the barre and stand in first position, begin to work on the posture of each student.

When posture is correct, the body can be likened to a tower of building blocks, one block stacked securely on another, head on top of the neck, neck on top of the shoulders, shoulders over hips, hips on top of legs, and knees over toes. The dancer appears vertical, but once she learns how to balance the body on the balls of the feet (see page 25), she will actually be positioned slightly forward of vertical, ready to take off like a rocket.

A light contraction of the abdominal muscles connects the upper body to the lower body. This action results in a C-curve when the body is viewed in profile. Ask a volunteer to stand at the barre facing sideways to the mirror with

Correct

Incorrect

the feet forming a narrow V. Place your hand on the student's back at the waist and ask her to gently try to touch your hand with her belly button. Very often this effort causes unnecessary tension in the neck and the arm. The challenge is to use the abdominal muscles without contracting the neck and the arm and to relax the neck and arm without relaxing the abdominal muscles.

Be careful using the phrase, "keep your back straight." In response, students may try to eliminate the natural curve of the buttocks by pushing the pelvis forward into the thighs. This action is commonly referred to as "tucking under," an action that works against rotation and balance.

To help students understand what it means to lengthen the spine against the force of gravity, pretend that the body is suspended from the ceiling by a string attached to the crown of the head.

Low fifth position of the working arm

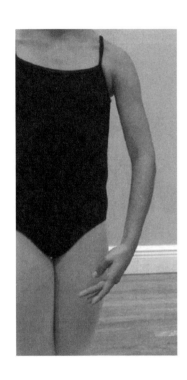

Most exercises are performed during the first year with the working arm in low fifth. Begin to refine this shape as soon as the class knows how to stand correctly with the feet in first position and the supporting hand on the barre.

Hold the arm a few inches away from the body and draw a letter C, half an oval, with no angles at the wrist or elbow. Rotate the upper arm inward without moving the shoulder. From the side the hand, elbow, and upper arm should fall on the same plane.

Balance

Try a simple experiment. Stand in first position with the full weight of the body over the heels, arm in low fifth. Now rise slowly to demi-pointe. You will notice that an ungainly shift occurs before the heels are able to lift off the floor. The body begins to fall backwards, and the muscles grip in response to this crisis. Now place all your weight on top of the balls of the feet. Notice how you are able to lift the heels straight up to demi-pointe without shifting and without tension.

This experiment is meant to demonstrate the importance of supporting the weight of the body on top of the balls of the feet during the execution of a ballet step. When moving through space, whether standing on one leg or two, understand that the ball of the foot is the last part of the body to leave and the first to return to the floor. It makes sense, therefore, to be poised on top of one or both of them, constantly prepared to move. Yes, the heels should touch the floor, but there is no reason for them to purposefully hold the weight of the body. Many teachers were horrified when they first heard that Balanchine was telling his dancers not to put their heels down. They believed all sorts of physical problems would result from this practice. He did not mean, though, to be perpetually en demi-point. He simply did not want the weight of the body falling back into the heels. He understood that dancers move quickly and efficiently only when they are on balance, on top of the legs.

To help students remember how to distribute the weight of the body, imagine a blue circle drawn on the ball of each foot and a red circle on each heel. Stand on the blue, stay off of the red! To encourage a constant awareness of how the weight is distributed, keeping the knees straight, bounce lightly on top of the blue circles before and after an exercise.

Pay attention to the way in which your students hold the barre. Ask your students to let go of the barre in the middle of an exercise and see what happens. Don't wait for the center to learn about balance. Take advantage of that important first half of class so that the transition to center will be seamless, not shocking.

Think of what it means to be off balance. How is it possible to stretch, co-ordinate parts of the body, be expressive, or even breathe when the body is struggling continuously to right itself? Think of the energy lost during recovery, the dangers of over-correcting. Observe how a boxer moves in the ring. Notice how he "dances" on the balls of his feet, fast, agile, and light, ready to move quickly into or away from his opponent.

Demi-plié in first position

The demi-plié is a source of power and a place of recovery.

Beginning with the feet parallel and the arm in low fifth, rotate the legs simultaneously to establish the V-shape of first position. Once posture, alignment, and balance are assessed, bend the knees as far as possible without lifting the heels and then straighten the knees.

Throughout the movement, remain balanced on top of the balls of the feet and use the abdominal muscles, the C-curve, to stabilize the pelvis. Hold the head on top of the neck, the chin lifted slightly and the eyes focused to the horizon. Pretend to balance a book on top of the head. Feel as if the body is suspended from the imaginary string as the body descends. Imagine a force pulling upward on that string when it comes time to straighten the knees.

Depending on the flexibility of the hips, rotation will increase somewhat as the knees bend and then reluctantly return to normal as the knees straighten. During those changes, make sure to keep the torso upright and the feet flat on the floor.

Note that the demi-plié is the best way to stretch the tendons in the back of the lower leg, tendons that are contracted repeatedly each time the foot is pointed or supports the body en demi-pointe. Because it is difficult to determine visually if a demi-plié is fully realized, always ask a dancer if she is bending her knees as far as possible. Describe a deep demi-plié as the basement. Look for the legs to shape a diamond.

Ask for a volunteer to perform the step. Let the class observe the volunteer from the front and from the side in order to make any necessary corrections. Demonstrate a demi-plié incorrectly and let the class fix you.

Grand plié in first position

Standing in first position, begin the grand plié by executing a demi-plié. At the moment the demi-plié reaches the basement, release the heels from the floor so that the knees can continue to bend. To come up, push the heels down to reach a demi-plié and then push through the balls of the feet to straighten the knees.

Think of the torso as a cereal box. Keep it upright as the knees bend and as they straighten. Balance a book on top of the head, look straight ahead, and keep the chin lifted slightly.

Pretend that the thighs are doors; open them as the body descends and try to keep them open as long as possible as the body returns to the starting position. At the bottom of the plié, make sure that the increase of rotation does not change the shape of the ankles.

Even though it is necessary to arrive at a specific place on a specific count of the music during the grand plié, move smoothly and without stopping. Accompany the grand plié using a slow triple-meter to encourage continuous movement. Count 1-&-a (demi-plié), 2-&-a (grand plié), 3-&-a (demi-plié), 4-&-a (straighten knees), using the stronger count of the triplet to indicate destination and the gentle pulses that follow to designate the journey.

The wave

The wave is a simple port de bras that teaches beginning students how to move the arms expressively. The movement begins in low fifth, opens to demi-seconde, and returns again to low fifth. Like a wave, it recedes before it is fully realized.

Pull the arm away from the body by moving the elbow to the side, stopping as it reaches the height of demi-seconde. From there, unfurl the forearm through the wrist and out the ends of the fingers.

Return the arm toward the body by bending the elbow slightly. To prevent the fingers from curling, pretend to pet the fur of a soft kitty with the fingertips. As soon as the elbow reaches its starting position, allow the forearm to fold into and complete the curve of low fifth.

Throughout the wave, draw the longest curve possible first under the arm and then on top. As the arm extends, prevent the elbow from locking even as the fingers extend. During the first year, move only the arm, keeping the head erect, the eyes front, and the shoulders level. A coordinating head movement will be added as the students advance to the second level.

The wave has the potential to become flowery and mannered, but it should be elegant and quiet. It should mirror the gentle inhalation and exhalation of a sigh. It should move with resistance, as if through water.

When students are ready, use this movement as a preparation for slow, fluid exercises. Hold the first and second counts, inhale and move the arm away from the body on the third count, exhale and return the arm to low fifth on the fourth count.

Grand plié in second position

Execute a grand plié in second position without lifting the heels. Bend the knees until the pelvis reaches a point even with or above knee-level and then return to standing. Open the thighs (the doors) and hold the torso (cereal box) upright.

Use anything you can think of to get your students to retain information. Repeating the information is effective but not necessarily the most interesting way of encouraging retention. Try to involve the students as much as you can. As soon as you give them information ask them to feed it back to you. Interrogate your students constantly. "Why do we do this?" "How do you do that?" "What's wrong with this?" "What's the name of that?" "Why does this happen?" Play games, have fun, and always be thrilled when you get the right answer or see a positive change.

Hyper-extension

If you notice that a student has hyper-extended legs, explain how to work with the problem, yet understand that it cannot be fixed easily or quickly. The difficulty lies in using the legs in different ways depending on whether they support the weight of the body or not. When a hyper-extended leg supports weight, in order to maintain alignment and prevent injury, the knee must not straighten, only appear straight. In the air, however, because there is no weight to support, the knee is free to stretch, drawing the beautiful curve that is characteristic of hyper-extension.

Correct

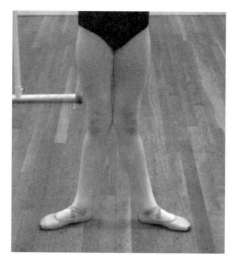

Incorrect

Demi-plié in second position

During a grand plié in second position, the pelvis is lowered to a point even with the knees. A demi-plié in second position descends to a point midway between standing and a full grand plié. Introduce the demi-plié after the grand plié so that students understand more easily where the mid-point lies.

Battement tendu à la seconde

Battement tendu à la seconde is the first step that requires a dancer to balance on one leg and draw a shape with the other. To differentiate one leg from the other, refer to the leg that holds the weight of the body as the standing or supporting leg and describe the leg that is free to move as the working leg.

Begin in first position with the weight on the balls of both feet. Slide the working foot along one side of the V shaped by the feet and at the same time begin to shift the weight over the ball (blue circle) of the supporting foot. Complete the shift as the working leg and foot stretch. Return the foot to first position along the same line of the V and finish with the weight equally distributed over the balls of both feet.

As a way to strengthen the foot and make it more flexible, roll through the foot when extending from and returning to first position. This process is the standing version of the flex/point exercise discussed earlier.

1. Slide the ball of the foot on the floor until the heel lifts as high as it can go and the top of the ankle stretches (demi-pointe).
2. Pointe tendue, lengthening the leg through the first three toes.
3. Place the ball of the foot on the floor, keeping the heel lifted and the top of the ankle stretched (demi-pointe).
4. Release the ankle, returning the heel to first position

Once the class understands how to roll through the foot, assign specific counts to each action. Work slowly, first without and then with music.

> Begin in first position with the arm in low fifth. Use the counts and pulses of a slow triple-meter. Slide the ball of the foot (&-a). With the ball of the foot on the floor, lift the heel as high as it can go to stretch the top of the ankle (1). Continue to stretch the top of the ankle (&-a). Pointe tendue à la seconde (2). Continue to lengthen the leg (&-a). With the ankle stretched and the heel lifted, lower the ball of the foot to the floor (3-&). Release the ankle (a). Close first position (4).

When concentrating specifically on how to roll through the foot, it is especially helpful to work barefoot or in socks. Naturally the foot needs support, especially in the center, but often, a dancer, even if advanced or professional, will gain new insights when the toes are free to spread out on the floor, moving into the tendu and releasing from it.

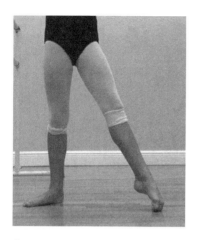

Incorrect

Never lean into the working foot when it is extended pointe tendue. Instead, touch the floor lightly with the tips of the toes. To test the balance of a dancer extending pointe tendue à la seconde, place your hand under the working foot and try to lift the leg. If it doesn't budge, you know that the weight has shifted off the supporting leg. Submit students to this test constantly. After a while, they will begin to evaluate their balance reflexively, whenever they see you coming.

Note that turn-out increases as the leg moves from a closed to an open position. If the working leg is extended in the proper direction and if the leg is rotated fully in the hip socket, the working heel should finish slightly in front of the foot.

When you ask a student to turn-out the working leg, always follow with a reminder to resist with the opposite side of the body (excluding the hand on the barre). Rotation cannot exist alone. The energy exerted in one direction must be balanced by an equal amount of energy exerted in the opposite direction. To illustrate this fact, demonstrate a modified leg circle, an exercise used in Pilates conditioning. Lie on the floor, knees bent and feet flat. Lift one leg to a ninety degree angle and point the foot. Make a small circle with the leg, but without moving the opposite side.

Once the class understands how to execute a battement tendu properly, use the step in combination with other movements.

> Begin in first position with the arm in low fifth. Use a slow triple-meter. Demi-plié (1-&)/straighten (a-2)/repeat (3-&)/(a-4)/grand plié (5-&-a, 6-&-a)/straighten (7-&-a,8)/port de bras to middle fifth (1-&-a,2-&-a)/low fifth (3-&-a,4)/battement tendu à la seconde (&-a-5,&-a-6)/first position (&-a-7,&-a-8). Repeat.

As the students progress, execute the battement tendu, using fewer counts. Slide the ball of the foot (&), keeping the ball of the foot on the floor, lift the heel and stretch the ankle (a), pointe tendue (1), continue to stretch the leg (&), lower the ball of the foot, keeping the heel lifted and the ankle stretched (a), return the heel to first position (2).

> Begin in first position with the arm in low fifth. Use a slow triple-meter. Battement tendu à la seconde (&-a-1-&)/first position (a-2)/battement tendu à la seconde (&-a-3-&)/first position (a-4)/battement tendu à la seconde (&-a-5-&)/first position (a-6)/demi-plié (7-&)/straighten (a-8). Repeat four times.

As a general rule, once the weight is safely on the ball of the supporting foot, it remains there unless there is a step within the exercise that requires the use of both legs or unless the exercise comes to an end. In the above exercise, shift the weight onto the ball of the foot as the working leg extends à la seconde and keep it there until the working leg closes in first position in preparation for the demi-plié.

Moving from first position to second and from second position to first

Moving the working leg from second position to and from pointe tendue à la seconde is sometimes difficult for beginners because the degree of rotation changes, depending on whether the foot is pointed or flat on the floor. The following transition from one shape to the other has proven successful for me over the years.

Start in first position. As the working foot slides along one side of the V, shift the weight of the body over the ball of the supporting foot. To place the working heel opposite the supporting foot in second position, move the working leg a little to the back just before rolling through the foot to lower the heel. Make sure the angles of both feet match.

To prevent the body from moving too far away from the barre, do not widen the stance as the foot is placed in second position. Instead, lower the heel directly from pointe tendue, shift the weight onto that leg, walk the inside leg closer to the barre, and redistribute the weight equally between both feet.

When making a transition from one position to another, rotate both legs with equal energy and keep the hips square. Make sure each position and each transition has a musical equivalent.

> Begin in first position with the arm in low fifth. Use a slow triple-meter. Demi-plié (1-&)/straighten (a-2)/repeat (3-&)/(a-4)/grand plié (5-&-a,6-&-a)/straighten (7-&-a,8-&-a)/repeat grand plié (1-4)/battement tendu à la seconde (&-a-5-&) second position (a-6)/the wave (7-&-a,8-&-a). Repeat the exercise in second position, returning to first position following the tendu.

Battement tendu quatrième devant

Introduce battement tendu quatrième devant as soon as the students are able to perform the battement tendu à la seconde correctly.

Start in first position and shift the weight onto the ball of the supporting foot as the working leg extends. To maintain the rotation of the working leg, lead the leg out of first position with the heel and return with the toes. Feel as if the foot is moving a brick to the front. Use your hand to hold back the lower part of a student's foot so that she has no choice but to move the heel first. Practice moving out and back to first with a flexed foot.

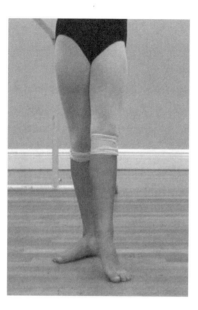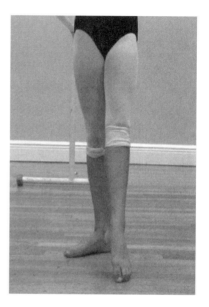

Keep the hips even and in line with the shoulders as the leg extends to the front. Pretend the pelvic bones are headlights and aim them to the front. Reach toward the floor through the big toe to shape the foot properly. To balance the stretch of the working leg, push through the ball (blue circle) of the supporting foot with equal energy.

> Begin in first position with the arm in low fifth. Use a slow triple-meter. Battement tendu quatrième devant (&-a-1-&)/first position (a-2)/repeat 2 times (&-a-3-&)/(a-4)/(&-a-5-&)/(a-6)/demi-plié (7-&)/straighten (a-8). Repeat 4 times.

In the previous exercise, shift the weight over the ball of the supporting foot during the first tendu, and keep it there until the end of the exercise.

Over time, increase the level of difficulty by combining steps and directions. For example, repeat the above combination à la seconde but instead of the demi-plié, execute the wave or lift the arm to middle fifth and then return it to low fifth. When the class is ready, combine both versions of the combination.

Elevé

The elevé is the first step that requires a dancer to stand on the balls of the feet. It is the basis of vertical movement.

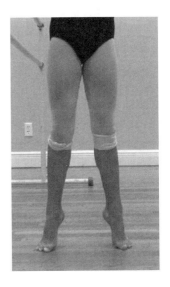

Start in first position with the hands resting lightly on the barre, eyes focused straight ahead. Stand on the blue circles, gently touching the floor with the red circles. Use the bounce test to determine if the weight is distributed correctly. Make sure that the rotation of the legs is shaping the position of the feet. If not, the legs will turn in as soon as the heels leave the floor.

Lift the heels off the floor as high as they can go, keeping the knees straight. Describe demi-pointe as the penthouse and contrast it to the demi-plié, the basement. At the top of the rise, make sure the ankles are aligned with the leg. Support the weight on the balls of the feet and the first three toes, with some weight on the last two toes depending on how the foot is structured. Demonstrate this placement without shoes.

Apply all the information concerning posture to the elevé. Balance a book on top of the head and stack the building blocks, one on top of the other. Imagine that the same string that was used previously to lengthen the spine and straighten the knees from a demi-plié now pulls the heels off the floor. Maintain the abdominal C-curve throughout the elevé. When the center is weak, the ribs will open as the heels lift off the floor, forcing the weight backwards. Think of the ribs as doors. Keep them closed!

When the class is able to execute the elevé correctly, combine the step with a demi-plié and add music.

I am always surprised at how such a small amount of material can be used in so many ways so soon. Be careful not to overwhelm the young mind. Balance the complex with the simple to find a median between confusion and boredom.

Begin in first position with both hands on the barre. Use a triple-meter. Demi-plié (1-&)/straighten (a-2)/elevé (3-&-a,4-&-a)/flat (5-&-a,6-&-a)/demi-plié (7-&)/straighten (a-8). Repeat 4 times.

Begin in first position with the arm in low fifth. Use a triple-meter. Demi-plié (1-&)/straighten (a-2)/repeat (3-&)/(a-4)/grand plié (5-&-a,6-&-a)/straighten (7-&-a,8)/elevé (1-&-a,2-&-a)/ flat (3-&-a,4)/battement tendu à la seconde (&-a-5-&)/first position (a-6)/repeat (&-a-7-&)/(a-8). Repeat 4 times.

Begin in first position with the arm in low fifth. Use a triple-meter. Battement tendu à la seconde (&-a-1-&)/first position (a-2)/repeat (&-a-3-&)/(a-4)/elevé (5-&-a,6-&-a)/flat (7-&-a,8). Repeat 4 times.

Begin in first position with the arm in low fifth. Use a triple-meter. Battement tendu quatrième devant (&-a-1-&)/first position (a-2)/demi-plié (3-&)/straighten (a-4)/elevé (5-&-a)/flat (6-&-a)/demi-plié (7-&)/straighten (a-8). Repeat à la seconde. Repeat all.

Normally, the knees straighten from a demi-plié on the count. To encourage students to keep the energy of the final position alive, in this case by pushing through the balls of the feet to lengthen the legs, vocalize the pulses (&-a) following the count.

Battement tendu à la seconde, duple-meter

Begin executing battement tendu à la seconde, using a slow duple-meter as soon as the students are able to maintain balance on the ball of the supporting foot and roll through and shape the working foot correctly.

> Begin in first position with both hands on the barre. Battement tendu à la seconde with the right foot (&-1)/first position (&-2)/repeat 2 times (3-6)/demi-plié (7)/straighten (8). Repeat to the other side. Repeat all.

In the above combination, lift the heel to stretch the top of the ankle on the pulse (&), preceding the first count. Lengthen the toes on the count (1). Lower the ball of the foot to the floor, continuing to stretch the top of the ankle, on the pulse (&) preceding the second count. Return the heel to first position on the count (2).

Demi-rond de jambe à terre

Students now have enough skills to execute a demi-rond de jambe à terre.

> Begin in first position with the arm in low fifth. Use a slow triple-meter. Battement tendu quatrième devant (&-a-1-&)/demi-rond de jambe à terre à la seconde (a-2-&)/first position (a-3)/hold (&-a-4-&-a)/demi-plié (5-&)/straighten (a-6)/demi-plié (7-&)/straighten (a-8). Repeat 4 times.

> Begin in first position with the arm in low fifth. Use a slow triple-meter. Battement tendu quatrième devant (&-a-1-&)/demi-rond de jambe à terre à la seconde (a-2-&)/first position (a-3)/hold (&-a-4-&-a)/repeat 2 times (5-8)/(1-4)/elevé (5-&)/flat (a-6)/ demi-plié (7-&)/straighten (a-8). Repeat all.

In the preceding exercises, make sure the working leg does not pull the body off balance. Maintain the weight of the body over the ball of the supporting foot until the working leg returns to first position. Reverse both exercises by extending the first tendu à la seconde and executing the demi-rond de jambe to the front.

Rotate the leg to move it from one position to another, heel in front of the foot, and keep all four corners of the cereal box intact.

Describe rond de jambe à terre as being en dedans or en dehors as soon as the step includes a movement of the leg to or from quatrième derrière. (see page 50).

Rolling through the foot to point en l'air

Learning how to roll the foot off the floor to a pointed position prepares for battement fondu, battement retiré, and, most importantly, the take off and landing of a jump. Practice this movement without shoes. Face sideways to the mirror and use a barre or chair for support. Students should be able to observe if the foot is shaping properly as it leaves the floor.

From first position, lift the heel as high as it will go (demi-pointe), shifting the weight over the ball of the supporting foot. Do not lift the toes off the floor, but mimic the action of jumping, pushing away from the floor to lengthen the foot. Describe the movement of the foot as a rocket exploding off a launch pad.

Already your students should begin to show the impressive results of your clear and careful teaching. Taking the time to lay a rich foundation will lighten your job as the class moves forward. You will reap the rewards of your patience and high standards.

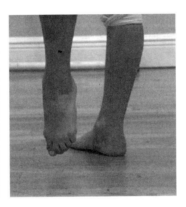

To return to first position, continue to stretch the ankle as the toes and the ball of the foot are placed on the floor. Press into the floor with the ball of the working foot but do not lean into it. Distribute the weight on the balls of both feet only when the heel is lowered.

To prevent the body from tilting away from the action of the working foot, think of the upper torso as a flowerpot sitting on a table. To keep the hips square, aim the pelvic bones (headlights) straight ahead.

In the following combinations, shape each position on the count.

Begin in first position with the arm in low fifth. Use a triple-meter. Lift heel (1-&-a)/point en l'air (2-&-a)/toes/ball (3-&-a)/heel (4). Repeat 8 times.

As students progress, use a slow duple-meter.

Lift heel (1)/point en l'air (2)/toes/ball (3)/heel (4). Repeat 8 times.

Using second position of the arm at the barre

The shape of this position is studied in the center during the beginning of the first year. Use the position at the barre only if low fifth interferes with the height or movement of the working leg.

Battement dégagé à la seconde

Introduce battement dégagé à la seconde once the students are able to execute a battement tendu à la seconde correctly in two counts of both a triple and duple-meter.

Stand in first position with an imaginary pencil placed perpendicular to the toes of the working foot. Press the ball of the working foot lightly into the floor and roll the pencil down one side of the V, shaped by first position. Use the action of the working foot to begin shifting the weight over the ball of the supporting foot. Just before the heel reaches its full height, brush the foot off the floor (shove the pencil), pulling the leg from the hip, stretching the back of the knee and the top of the ankle, and completing the transfer of weight. Note that the working leg will lift off the floor somewhat, not purposefully from the hip, but as a reaction to the shove.

To return to first position, remember to stretch the ankle as the tips of the toes and the ball of the foot release into the floor. Release the ankle only to lower the heel.

Use sound effects to illustrate the dynamics of the movement, to show the difference between the foot sliding and taking off and then gliding back into first. Use words like massage, rub, and caress to illustrate how the foot interacts with the surface of the floor.

During the first year, execute the dégagé in two counts, one out and one in. By the second year, the class should be able to begin on the pulse (&) preceding the count, however, the tempo should still be slow enough to allow for a clear articulation of the foot.

> Begin in first position with the arm in low fifth. Use a duple-meter. Begin to slide the ball of the foot (1)/dégagé (2)/toes/ball (3)/first position (4). Repeat 8 times.

> Begin in first position with the arm in low fifth. Use a slow duple-meter. Battement dégagé à la seconde (&-1)/first position (&-2)/repeat (&-3)/(&-4)/lift heel (5)/point en l'air (6)/toes/ball (7)/lower heel(8). Repeat 4 times.

Battement tendu à la seconde, flexing and pointing

Flex and point the foot within a combination whenever possible, not only to increase the flexibility of the foot and the calf but to develop the ability to draw a straight line with the leg by stretching the knee and the top of the ankle at the same time.

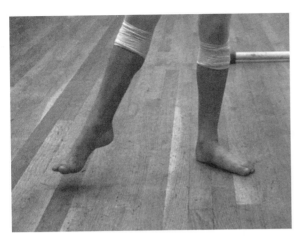 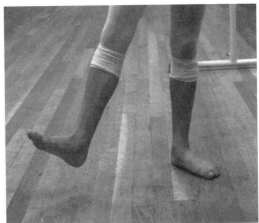

Begin in first position with the arm in low fifth. Use a slow triple-meter. Battement tendu à la seconde (&-a-1-&)/adjust working leg (a)/lower the ball of the foot (2-&)/heel flat in second position (a-3-&)/lift heel (a-4-&)/adjust working leg to pointe tendue à la seconde (a-5-&)/first position (a-6)/demi-plié (7-&)/straighten (a-8). Repeat 4 times.

Begin in first position with the arm in low fifth. Use a slow duple-meter. Battement tendu à la seconde (&-1)/flex the toes (2)/flex the ankle (3)/stretch the top of the ankle (4)/pointe tendu (5)/first position (&-6)/demi-plié (7)/straighten (8). Repeat 8 times.

Battement tendu relevé à la seconde

In a previous discussion, it was noted that because the beginning student is usually unable to extend a battement tendu directly to the side of the body, a small adjustment of the working leg is required when moving from a battement tendu à la seconde to second position flat. The working leg must move back so that both heels are able to line up when the working heel lowers to the floor. This same action is reversed when the leg moves from second position to pointe tendue à la seconde. The working leg adjusts forward slightly and turns in the hip socket to bring the heel in front of the foot. Apply this information when introducing battement tendu relevé à la seconde.

Begin in first position with the arm in low fifth. Use a slow triple-meter. Battement tendu à la seconde (&-a-1-&)/adjust working leg (a)/lower the ball of the foot (2-&-a)/lower the heel to second position (3-&-a)/lift heel (4-&-a)/adjust working leg to pointe tendue à la seconde (5-&)/first position (a-6)/demi-plié (7-&)/straighten (a-8). Repeat 4 times.

Shift the weight over the ball of the supporting leg as the working foot slides à la seconde. When the working heel lowers to second position, distribute the weight equally on the balls of both feet. When the working foot pushes away from the floor to pointe tendue à la seconde, again, shift the weight back onto the ball of the supporting foot but distribute the weight equally on both feet as the working leg returns to first position before the demi-plié. Make sure to keep the hips square during each adjustment.

> Begin in first position with the arm in low fifth. Use a slow duple-meter. Battement tendu à la seconde (&-1)/adjust working leg and lower the heel to second position (&-2)/roll through the foot and adjust the working leg to pointe tendue à la seconde (&-3)/first position (&-4). Repeat 8 times.

In the above exercise, move the weight over the ball of the supporting foot each time the working leg extends pointe tendu à la seconde. Distribute the weight equally on both feet in second and first positions.

> Begin in first position with the arm in low fifth. Use a duple-meter. Battement tendu relevé à la seconde (&-1,&-2,&-3)/first position (&-4)/battement tendu à la seconde (&-5)/first position (&-6)/repeat (&-7)/(&-8). Repeat 4 times.

At the end of the above exercise, do not distribute the weight equally on both feet in first position. Instead, keep the weight over the ball of the supporting foot, ready to repeat the sequence.

Relevé

In preparation for a relevé that springs into position and for a sauté from first position, introduce a relevé that rolls up to and down from demi-pointe.

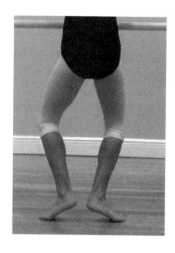

> Begin in first position with both hands on the barre. Use a triple-meter. Demi-plié (1-&)/lift the heels slightly off the floor and begin to straighten the knees (a)/straighten both knees as the heels lift as high as they can go (demi-pointe) (2)/hold (&-a)/ begin to bend the knees (3) lower the heels (&)/straighten (a-4). Repeat 4 times.

Each movement of a roll-up relevé both causes and overlaps the next. On the rise, the knees straighten because the heels lift. On the descent, the heels lower because the knees bend.

Stand on top of the balls of the feet in the starting position, and as the knees bend, widen the thighs against a stable core to shape a diamond. To maintain rotation as the heels leave the floor, make sure the angles of the feet in the starting position are determined by the rotation of the legs in the hip sockets.

Rolling up, rest the hands lightly on the barre to feel how the body is balanced and contract the abdominals to connect the upper body to the lower body. Like an express elevator, move between the basement and the penthouse, smoothly and continuously, without stopping.

Introduce a spring relevé once the class can roll up and down through demi-pointe with no loss of alignment. The spring relevé uses the feet and legs in the same way as a roll-up relevé but the movement is quicker, and the demi-plié is used not only to lift the body up to demi-pointe but up and onto the legs as well. To spring into a relevé means to leave the floor. This movement is not a jump, but at one point it should be possible to pass a piece of paper under the feet. The energy used to spring is the same that will one day move the dancer onto point.

> Begin in first position with both hands on the barre. Use a staccato duple-meter. Demi-plié (&-1)/relevé (2)/demi-plié (&-3)/straighten (&-4). Repeat 4 times.

In the above combination, begin to bend the knees on the pulse (&) preceding the first count. Reach the basement on the first count. Begin to lift the heels on the pulse (&) preceding the second count. Reach demi-pointe on the second count. Begin to bend the knees on the pulse (&) preceding the third count. Lower the heels on the third count. Begin to straighten the knees on the pulse (&) before the fourth count. Straighten the knees on the fourth count.

Use your voice to illustrate the connection as well as the dynamic contrast between the movements. Accent the second count but draw out all the others.

Battement soutenu

Battement soutenu lays the foundation for pas de bourrée dessous and glissade derrière, teaching how to move the body standing on one leg.

Practice the following exercises to prepare for battement soutenu. Remember to shift the weight as the working leg extends.

> Begin in first position with the arm in low fifth. Use a slow triple-meter. Battement tendu à la seconde (&-a-1-&)/fondu (a-2-&)/straighten (a-3-&)/first position (a-4). Repeat 4 times.

> Begin in first position with the arm in low fifth. Use a slow triple-meter. Demi-plié (1-&)/battement tendu à la seconde en fondu (a-2-&)/demi-plié first position (a-3-&)/straighten (a-4). Repeat 4 times.

Begin the battement soutenu from first position and on the first count, execute a battement tendu à la seconde en fondu. On the second count, straighten the standing knee and at the same time, return the working leg to first position.

> Begin in first position with the arm in low fifth. Use a slow duple-meter. Battement tendu à la seconde (&-1) first position (&-2) repeat 2 times (3-6)/battement sountenu close first position (&-7)/(&-8). Repeat 4 times.

In the above exercise, shift the weight over the ball of the supporting foot as the working leg extends and maintain the weight over the ball of the supporting foot until the end of the exercise. Remember, whenever you think a dancer is not working on top of the standing leg, ask her let go of the barre and lift the working leg off the floor.

Dégagé en l'air à la seconde

Start from first position and shift the weight over the ball of the supporting foot as the working leg extends. Move through pointe tendue à la seconde before

Correct

Incorrect

and after the dégagé en l'air in order to give the dancers an opportunity to check on their balance and alignment and to make sure that the working leg is fully rotated with the leg in front of the body, heel in front of the foot. Until rotation, alignment, and balance can be maintained consistently, lift the leg only a few inches.

Adding a preparation of the arm to second position is appropriate at this time, if the class is ready. If not, prepare the arm to middle fifth.

Make sure that the body resists the action of the working leg. Keep the headlights even and aimed to the front and don't let the flowerpot tilt.

> Begin in first position with the arm in low fifth. Use a slow triple-meter. Prepare the arm to second position through middle fifth on the last two counts of the preparation. Battement tendu à la seconde (&-a-1-&)/dégagé en l'air (a-2-&)/pointe tendue à la seconde (a-3-&)/first position (a-4)/ demi-plié (5-&)/roll-up relevé (a-6-&-a)/demi-plié (7-&)/straighten (a-8). Repeat 4 times.

In the above combination, begin to lift the leg on the pulse (a) before the count (2) and begin to lower the leg on the pulse (a) in order to pointe tendue à la seconde on the count (3).

> Begin in first position with the arm in low fifth. Use a slow triple-meter. Prepare the arm to second position through middle fifth on the last two counts of the preparation. Battement tendu à la seconde (&-a-1-&)/dégagé en l'air (a-2-&)/pointe tendue à la seconde (a-3-&)/first position (a-4)/ elevé (5-&-a)/flat (6-&-a)/demi-plié (7-&)/straighten (a-8). Repeat 4 times.

Begin in first position with the arm in low fifth. Use a triple-meter. Prepare the arm to second position through middle fifth on the last two counts of the preparation. Battement tendu quatrième devant (&-a-1-&)/demi-rond de jambe à la seconde (a-2-&)/first position (a-3)/hold (&-a-4)/battement tendu à la seconde (&-a-5-&)/dégagé en l'air (a-6-&)/ pointe tendue à la seconde (a-7-&)/first position (a-8). Repeat 4 times.

Attitude à la seconde

Introduce attitude à la seconde once the dancers are able to execute a dégagé en l'air à la seconde at 45 degrees.

It has already been noted that the rotation of the legs in the hip socket increases when both knees bend (demi-plié) or when one leg moves away from the body (battement tendu à la seconde). A similar increase occurs when a straight leg, held en l'air, bends. And just as the heel moves in front of the foot during the transition from first position to pointe tendue à la seconde, so the lower half of the leg moves slightly in front of the thigh when moving from dégagé en l'air à la seconde to attitude à la seconde.

Begin in first position with the arm in low fifth. Use a triple-meter. Prepare the arm to second position through middle fifth on the last two counts of the preparation. Battement tendu à la seconde (&-a-1-&)/dégagé en l'air (a-2-&)/attitude (a-3-&)/extend (a-4-&)/pointe tendue (a-5-&)/first position (a-6)/demi-plié (7-&)/straighten (a-8). Repeat 4 times.

Correct

Incorrect

To resist the movements of the working leg, keep the flowerpot on the table and the hips square. Maintain balance by pressing into the floor through the ball of the supporting foot.

Beginning and ending an exercise

A dancer, waiting in the wings before her variation, must be calm, focused, physically aware, and listening closely for the musical cue that tells her when to make her entrance. At the end of her dance, she holds her final pose so that the audience knows it is time to acknowledge her performance and the pleasure they received from it.

Observe these same rituals in the classroom. As your students wait for an exercise to begin, remind them to take measure of alignment and balance, the shape of the arm, the focus of the eyes, and the height of the chin. When the exercise comes to an end, expect them to hold the final position, to recover from and in recognition for the effort they have made.

Fifth position of the feet

Although many teachers work from third position during the first year, I prefer to introduce fifth as soon as the class is working with strength and assurance from first position.

Correct

As with all positions, the angles of the feet in fifth position are determined by the rotation of the legs. And because both legs are required to rotate with equal energy to keep the body on balance and in balance whether standing or moving, then both feet should be placed on the floor at equal angles in fifth position. To illustrate this point, draw a line perpendicular to the barre and stand on the line in fifth position. If the feet are placed correctly the line will bisect the V-shape formed by the feet.

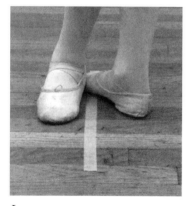

Incorrect

Advanced as well as beginning students often rotate the front foot more than the back leg in order to appear more turned-out in fifth position. As a result, the front foot pronates, rolls over, an action that can, over time, weaken or injure the ankle as well as the knee. From the start, emphasize that fifth position has nothing to do with how tight the feet fit together, but everything to do with how much the legs rotate in the hip socket.

With beginners, it is not necessary for the toes of the back foot and the heel of the front foot to touch. Because of leg shape, very often it is easier to feel rotation in the top of the leg when the heel and toe are separated by a small space. This space will prove especially valuable once the students begin to learn how to point the foot in back of the ankle, moving from fifth position back.

Because the balls of the feet are so close to the mid-line standing in fifth position, it is possible to place the weight of the body over the ball of what is to be the standing leg before the working leg even leaves the starting position. Starting a movement on balance is always safer and more efficient than shifting the weight as a movement begins.

Introduce a demi-plié in fifth position as soon as students are able to shape the feet correctly and with ease. Use fifth position and demi-plié in fifth position when applicable but continue to introduce new steps from first position.

Battement frappé à la seconde

While the working foot may be wrapped or flexed at the start of a battement frappé, the flexed position is best for beginning students. When the foot is flexed, it is easier to move the working leg in the hip socket and to feel if the toes are lined up with the knee.

Practice moving to the flexed position from battement tendu à la seconde. Bend the working knee and place the outside edge of the flexed foot on the supporting ankle so that the working heel extends a bit beyond the supporting leg. Touch the supporting leg lightly. Do not use the supporting leg as leverage to achieve rotation.

Shape the foot without tension, maintaining an angle of more than ninety degrees between the ankle and the top of the working foot so that the ball of the foot is positioned to move into the floor close to the supporting heel. Allow the toes to continue the line of the foot. Make sure they do not curl in anticipation of the frappé.

Again, use the image of a pencil lying perpendicular to the working foot. Push the pencil in the direction of the working knee and just before the knee

Correct

Correct

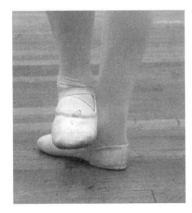

Incorrect

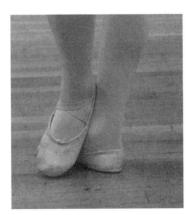

Incorrect

extends, give the pencil a shove. As with the battement dégagé, use the energy coming from the shove to stretch the top of the ankle, the toes, and the back of the knee. Make a sound such as shhhhhhump to give voice to the slide/shove action of the frappé. Let the students make the same sound as they execute the step.

Striking the floor with the tips of the toes is another way to execute a battement frappé. This method supports the literal meaning of the step and is intended to develop the ability to point the foot quickly. While brushing the foot off the floor contradicts the meaning of the step, it also develops the ability to point quickly with an added bonus of making the foot stronger and suppler by bringing all the joints into play. Later, when the dancers perform such steps as the jeté and the assemblé, you will see that the power of the jump is doubled when the ball of the working foot brushes off the floor at the same time as the ball of the supporting foot pushes off. Striking the floor with the tips of the toes provides no such assistance.

As the working knee bends to return the foot to the ankle, resist the increased rotation of the working thigh by keeping the hips square. The working foot may graze the floor, but should not do so intentionally.

> Begin in first position with the arm in low fifth. Use a duple-meter. Battement tendu à la seconde (&-1)/ flex devant (2)/ frappé à la seconde (&-3)/ first position (&-4). Repeat 8 times.

> Begin in first position with the arm in low fifth. Use a duple-meter. Battement tendu à la seconde (&-1)/ flex devant (2)/ frappé à la seconde (&-3)/ flex devant (4)/ frappé à la seconde (&-5)/ tendu à la seconde (6)/ first position (&-7)/ hold (8). Repeat 4 times.

  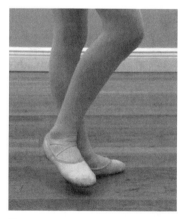

Correct   *Correct*   *Incorrect*

Since the shape of the flexed foot both in front and in back of the ankle are identical, teach the class how to shape the flexed position in back by moving the flexed foot from the front to the back. Be sure the starting position of the working leg is aligned correctly, knee over toes, heel in front of foot.

Keeping the hips even, rotate the leg in the hip socket, opening the thigh, to move the foot from front to back. Note that the rotation that exerts outward pressure on the thigh should be ever-present, shaping the leg in front of the ankle, in back of the ankle, moving the leg from the front to the back, and holding the shape of the leg when the foot returns from the back to the front.

When the foot is flexed at the back of the supporting ankle, surround the bottom of the calf with the inside of the working ankle, making sure to maintain the alignment of the knee and the toes.

During the frappé, contact the floor with the inside of the ball of the foot and slide it diagonally in the direction of the working knee. At the end of the movement, finish à la seconde with the heel in front of the foot.

Practice moving from a battement tendu à la seconde to a flexed position in back of the ankle once the shape of the position is understood.

> Begin in first position with the arm in low fifth. Use a duple-meter. Battement tendu à la seconde (&-1)/flex derrière (2)/frappé à la seconde (&-3)/ first position (&-4). Repeat 8 times.

> Begin in first position with the arm in low fifth. Use a duple-meter. Battement tendu à la seconde (&-1)/flex devant (2)/battement frappé à la seconde (&-3)/ first position (&-4)/battement tendu à la seconde (&-5)/flex derrière (6)/battement frappé à la seconde (&-7)/first position (&-8). Repeat 4 times.

> Begin in first position with the arm in low fifth. Use a duple-meter. Battment tendu à la seconde (&-1)/flex devant (2)/battement frappé à la seconde (&-3)/flex derrière (4)/battement frappé à la seconde (&-5)/flex devant (6)/battement frappé à la seconde (&-7)/first position (&-8). Reverse and repeat all.

Grand battement à la seconde in four counts

Like the dégagé en l'air, begin and end the grand battement from pointe tendue à la seconde in order to give students time to assess the shape of each position. Again, the leg should lift off the floor only a few inches until the students are able to keep the heel in front of the foot, the hips square, and the flowerpot sitting on the table. When ready, encourage students to increase extension but never at the expense of alignment, balance, or rotation.

If the step begins in first position, shift the weight onto the ball of the

When accented movements are performed with the leg, other parts of the body often react by tensing or jerking. To bring this problem to the attention of the students, practice an exercise with the working arm hanging to the side of the body, without shape and totally relaxed. Only if the center is strong enough to absorb the energy of the frappé, will the arm remain still.

supporting foot as the working leg extends pointe tendue à la seconde. Make sure the weight of the body does not fall into the working foot as it descends from the grand battement. Touch the floor lightly before closing first position.

Despite the height limitation, try to achieve a contrast between the way the leg lifts and the way it lowers. Ring a bell on the way up and then let the leg float down like a feather.

> Begin in first position with the arm in low fifth. Use a March or Tango. Prepare the arm to second position through middle fifth on the last two counts of the preparation. Battement tendu à la seconde (&-1)/grand battement (2)/pointe tendue à la seconde (&-3)/first position (&-4). Repeat 4 times.

During the &-counts in the exercises above, remember to stretch the top of the ankle moving into and returning from the tendu. When the class is ready, eliminate the fourth battement and add instead demi-plié (1)/relevé (2)/demi-plié (3)/straighten (4).

Battement tendu quatrième derrière

It is essential that battement tendu quatrième derrière be taught correctly. It is the basis of the arabesque. Pull a barre or chair out into center and work on this position, facing sideways to the mirror to enable the student to study the line of the leg. Work with each student individually.

Starting in first position, lead the foot to the back with the toes and return with the heel, the reverse of battement tendu quatrième devant. To create the correct line with the leg, make sure the knee faces out, never down. Use the image of a smiley face, drawn on the kneecap and ever visible from the side, as

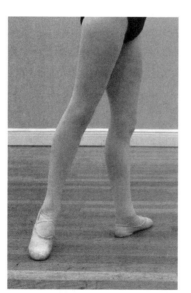

evidence of a rotated leg. Make sure the working heel cannot be seen from the side.

Keep the foot shaped and aligned with the leg as it moves in and out of first position. Rotate the leg and, as the toes open, contact the floor with only the inside of the ball of the foot and the big toe. At the end of the tendu, as the top of the ankle stretches and the toes lengthen, touch the floor with only the tip of the big toe, the corner of the toenail. From pointe tendue, keep the top of the ankle stretched and release the toes, setting the inside of the ball of the foot and the inside of the big toe on the floor. Rotate to move the leg, pulling the inner thigh and the heel back to first position.

Because the pelvis is not constructed in a way that allows the leg to extend behind the body and rotate, two adjustments are necessary. First, as the leg extends and the weight moves onto the ball of the supporting foot, shift the torso forward and up so that the pelvis is positioned to accommodate the direction of the leg. Second, use the maximum rotation of the leg to spiral the pelvis slightly and open the hip. In this way, the aesthetic line is achieved; the knee is visible from the side but the heel is not. Both adjustments should be subtle and should be made, not in anticipation of the extension of the leg, but in response to it. Neither should they be allowed to destabilize the body. To make sure the supporting side develops enough strength to resist the actions of the working side, hold the barre lightly.

Correct   *Incorrect*

Beginning students often hyper-extend the lumbar spine as the working leg moves to the back. The ribs open, the tummy protrudes, and the upper body falls behind the hips. A straight line should extend diagonally from under the breast down to the big toe of the working leg. Pretend to zip up tight jeans as a way to scoop up the lower abdominal muscles. Think of the rib cage as a set of doors and keep them closed. Picture the body as a seesaw, the head and torso on one side and the leg on the other.

Make sure that the hand moves along the barre when the torso adjusts forward. If the hand is fixed, a forward adjustment is prevented, and hyper-extension of the back will become the only option.

Rond de jambe à terre in four counts

Once battement tendu quatrième derrière is mastered, introduce demi-rond de jambe à terre to and from that position followed by rond de jambe à terre in four counts, both en dehors and en dedans.

Introduce and discuss the difference between the terms, "en dehors" and "en dedans". Think of first position as a door. During a rond de jambe en dehors, move the working leg out the door and during a rond de jambe en dedans, move the leg in through the door.

> Begin in first position with the arm in low fifth. Use a slow triple-meter. Prepare the arm to second position through middle fifth on the last two counts of the preparation. Battement tendu quatrième devant (&-a-1-&)/ demi-rond de jambe à la seconde (a-2-&)/demi-rond de jambe quatrième devant (a-3-&)/first position (a-4)/repeat 2 times (5-8)/(1-4)/lift heel (5)/point en l'air (6)/ toes/ball (7)/heel (8). Reverse and repeat all.

If an exercise finishes with the arm in second position, return the arm to low fifth in order to signify the completion of the exercise. Transitioning from second to low fifth will be discussed in the section devoted to first year center work.

When the leg is extended to the front and carried to the side, keep the body upright, but when the working leg moves a little past its position à la seconde on its way to quatrième derrière, respond as you would to a battement tendu quatrième derrière. Shift the torso forward so that the leg is able to move to the back and open the hip slightly so that the leg is able rotate in the hip socket. Deepen the C-curve and hold the ribs together to support the lower back.

Maintain a connection between the side arm and the shoulder and slide the hand forward on the barre as the torso shifts forward in space. Return the side arm and the hand on the barre to their original positions when the working leg returns to first position and vertical alignment is restored.

> Begin in first position with the arm in low fifth. Use a slow triple-meter. Prepare the arm to second position through middle fifth on the last two counts of the preparation. Battement tendu quatrième devant (&-a-1-&)/ demi-rond de jambe à la second (a-2-&)/demi-rond de jambe quatrième derrière (a-3-&)/first position (a-4)/elevé (5-&-a)/flat (6-&-a)/demi-plié (7-&)/straighten (a-8). Repeat 2 times and reverse.

Moving the foot from fifth position front to point sur le cou-de-pied devant

Before more complex steps such as a battement retiré and battement fondu are introduced, it is necessary to learn how to move the foot from fifth position front to point sur le cou-de-pied devant.

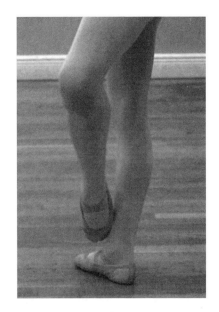

Begin standing in fifth position. Make sure the angles of the feet are equal and place the weight of the body on top of the ball of the supporting foot (the back foot) in anticipation of the action of the working foot. Lift the working heel of the front foot as high as it can go. Without leaning on the ball of the foot, press through the first three toes and gently push away from the floor. As the foot points en l'air, guide the little toenail to the ankle. Note how the thigh is able to open wider as soon as the working foot is free of the confines of fifth position.

To return to fifth position front, move the pointed foot over the original footprint of the starting fifth. Roll through the foot into the footprint, making sure that the toes release as the foot folds into the floor, not in anticipation of the floor. Maintain the weight over the ball of the supporting foot if the movement is to be repeated. If not, finish the exercise with the weight equally distributed on both feet.

> Begin in fifth position with the arm in low fifth. Use a slow triple-meter. Prepare the arm to middle fifth on the last count of the preparation or to second position through middle fifth on the last two counts of the preparation. Lift the heel (1-&,a-2-&)/point en l'air (a)/sur le cou-de-pied devant (3-&,a-4-&)/move the foot over the footprint (a) toes/ball (5-&-a,6-&)/ heel (a-7)/hold (&-a-8). Repeat 4 times.

Moving from cou-de-pied devant to cou-de-pied derrière
During the second year, the class will learn how to move from fifth position back to point sur le cou-de-pied derrière. Until then, teach students to point in back of the ankle by moving the foot from cou-de-pied devant to cou-de-pied derrière.

Ask a volunteer to point the foot sur le cou-de-pied devant. Place the palm of your hand on the inside of her thigh, close to the knee, and gently push it back. Use the image of opening a door as the outward pressure on the thigh pulls the foot to the back of the calf. Note that the working thigh will automatically turn inward if the foot moves first.

While the shape of the ankle never changes as the foot moves from one position to another, the point of contact between the working foot and the

 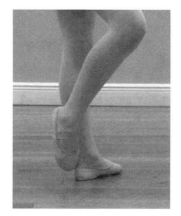

Correct   *Incorrect*

standing leg does change. When the working foot is positioned in front, the toe-nail of the little toe touches the ankle. When it is positioned in back, the inside of the working heel lightly touches the lower calf of the supporting leg.

To move from back to front, reverse the action. Initiate the return with the lower leg or heel, resisting with the top of the thigh or knee. To return the foot to fifth position, remember to move the toes over the starting footprint before folding the foot into the floor.

> Begin in fifth position with the arm in low fifth. Use a slow triple-meter. Lift the heel (1-&)/point en l'air (a)/sur le cou-de-pied devant (2-&)/sur le cou-de-pied derrière (a-3)/hold (&-a-4-&)/ sur le cou-de-pied devant (a-5)/ hold (&-a-6-&)/move the foot over the footprint (a) toes/ball (7-&)/heel (a-8). Repeat 4 times.

When ready, repeat the above combination using a slow duple-meter.

> Begin in fifth position with the arm in low fifth. Point sur le cou-de-pied devant (&-1)/sur le cou-de-pied derrière (&-2)/sur le cou-de-pied devant (&-3)/move the foot over the footprint (&)/fifth position (a-4). Repeat 8 times.

Repeat the above exercise three times and combine with a grand battement in four counts, closing fifth position front to allow for another repetition.

Battement retiré devant

As soon as the class is able to move the foot from fifth position to point sur le cou-de-pied devant, introduce battement retiré devant. With the hips square, slide the little toenail from the ankle up the shin to a point just below the knee. This is a reasonable foot placement for beginners. Once the flexibility of the hip joint increases and the supporting muscles of the back, leg, and hip are strong

Correct   *Correct*

As you continue to teach students how to change the position of the working foot from one place to another on the supporting leg, you will notice certain patterns emerging. First, the shape of the foot, whether flexed, pointed, or wrapped, placed at the knee, or at the ankle stays the same when moving from front to back, back to front, or up and down. Second, rotation of the working leg moves the foot from the front to the back. And third, the rotation of the supporting leg resists the movement of the foot from the back to the front.

enough to keep the pelvis stable, the foot may be lifted higher.

To return the working leg to fifth position, slide the little toenail down the shin to the ankle and separate the foot from the leg so that it can fold into the starting footprint of fifth position.

To prevent leaning towards or away from the working leg, use the image of the flowerpot. To keep the hips even as the thigh rotates, aim the headlights to the front.

Incorrect   *Incorrect*

Sinking into the supporting hip will occur if the supporting leg fails to rotate. Show how the front of the thigh flattens and the back of the thigh tightens when the leg turns or wraps in the hip socket. Be aware that it takes a long time to develop enough strength to truly support with the supporting leg.

> Begin in fifth position with the arm in low fifth. Use a slow triple-meter. Prepare the arm to middle fifth on the last count of the preparation or to second position through middle fifth on the last two counts of the preparation. Lift the heel (1-&)/point en l'air (a)/sur le cou-de-pied devant (2-&)/retiré devant (a-3-&)/sur le cou-de-pied devant (a-4-&)/move the foot over the footprint (a)/toes/ball (5-&)/ heel (a-6)/demi-plié (7-&)/straighten (a-8). Repeat 4 times.

Soussus

The ability to maintain posture and stand solidly on demi-pointe during a relevé from first signifies a readiness to learn the soussus.

Begin by analyzing the shape of a fifth position demi-pointe in front of the mirror. First, move to an open fifth by raising the heels straight up from fifth position flat. From the open fifth on demi-pointe, shift the weight onto the back foot and, at the same time, slide the front foot into a closed fifth, shaping one foot with two heels. Distribute the weight of the body equally on both feet.

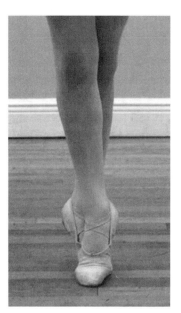

Standing in this position with eyes closed, feel those points where the legs make contact. Next, practice a relevé from fifth position demi-plié to fifth position demi-pointe, making sure that the legs make contact at those same points.

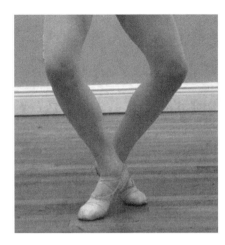 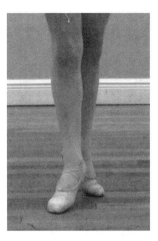

To execute a demi-plié from fifth position demi-pointe, shift the weight onto the back foot, open the front leg, placing the ball of the foot over the footprint of fifth position, and then bend the knees to lower the heels.

When everyone is able to successfully shape fifth position on demi-pointe and return to a demi-plié fifth position, perform the following exercise.

Begin in fifth position with the right foot front, both hands on the barre. Use a slow triple-meter. Demi-plié (1-&-a)/soussus (2) separate the front leg from the back leg (a)/demi-plié fifth position, right foot front (3-&)/straighten (a-4). Repeat 4 times.

Wait until the second year to bring the soussus to the center.

3 IN THE CENTER

During the beginning of the first year, there is often no distinct division between the barre and the center. The class moves back and forth between the two, not only to accommodate the material being presented, but to keep interest alive. As your students progress, however, the class takes on a more traditional form. The number of barre exercises increases and center floor work expands to include those exercises from the barre that have been mastered.

Floor stretches

Use floor stretches to give the students a break between the barre and the center or as a cool-down at the end of class.

The following exercises are appropriate for dancers of all levels. They are designed to increase flexibility or release tight muscles, all within the context of proper alignment. It is not necessary to incorporate all these exercises in every class. Do as many as time allows but vary your choices so that all parts of the body are addressed at one time or another.

Teach the dancers to exhale and relax into a stretch. Discourage bouncing, holding the breath, gripping or anything that might inhibit a stretch.

1. Head and neck

Sit on the floor with the soles of the feet together, hands resting lightly on the legs, back straight, head erect and eyes front. Tilt the head to the right and circle it, bringing the chin over, but not touching, the mid-line. Continue to circle the head until it tilts to the left and then bring the head erect. Keep the shoulders level and down as the head moves on top of the neck. Repeat the exercise, starting left.

2. Shoulders

Sit on the floor cross-legged, holding a towel with both hands, arms extended in a wide V in front of the chest. Keeping the back straight and the ribs closed, bring the towel over and behind the head to open the chest and stretch the arms in the shoulder sockets.

3. Spine

Sit cross-legged on the floor with the back straight and the arms extended to the side, palms down. Inhale to prepare, exhale to spiral the upper body from the waist to face the knee, inhale to return the upper body to the front, and exhale to repeat the spiral to the other side. Move the upper body as a unit, arms with the shoulders, head with the body, and eyes with the head.

4. *Lower back*

Lie on the floor with the feet flat and the knees bent. Lift the feet and clasp the knees with the hands. Keeping the back pressed against the floor, exhale and pull both knees toward the shoulders. Continuing to hold the knees, release the stretch and inhale. Repeat five times and relax. During a second set, allow the lower back to curve off the floor as the knees move toward the shoulders.

5. *Lower back*

On hands and knees sit back on the heels. With the arms extended on the floor, let the chest lie on the thighs. Relax into the shape, breathing easily. This is a yoga position called the "child's pose."

6. *Lower back and rotators*

Lie on the floor with the feet flat and the knees bent. Bring one knee toward the chest and cross the foot of the other leg over the top of the bent knee, making sure the pelvis is squarely aligned. Reach one hand through the triangle formed by both legs and clasp the other hand under the thigh. Gently pull the thigh toward the chest with both hands and exhale. This exercise releases those muscles that contract during rotation.

7. Lower back and hips

Sit on the floor with a straight back, soles of the feet together and the legs in the shape of a diamond. Bring the forehead toward the feet as if rounding over a barrel. Maintain an abdominal C-curve to protect the lower back. Roll up to return upright.

8. Inner thighs

Lie on the floor with the feet flat and the knees bent. Unfold one leg and then the other until both extend perpendicular to the floor, feet pointed. Rotate the legs and holding the inside of the thighs, open them to the side. Keeping the back flat to prevent the lower back from arching, exhale for three counts and let gravity deepen the stretch. Return the legs to a perpendicular position, rotate inward, and return one foot at a time to the floor. Repeat the exercise with the feet flexed.

9. *Hamstrings*

Lie on the floor with the feet flat and the knees bent. Keeping the hips even, bring one knee toward the chest until the thigh is perpendicular to the floor. Clasping the hands under the thigh, unfold the bottom half of the leg to the knee and flex the foot. Pull the leg toward the chest until a gentle stretch is felt. Exhale into the stretch for three counts then release the knee. Repeat three times, first with the foot flexed and then with the foot pointed. Repeat all with the other leg.

10. *Hamstrings*

Sit on the floor with the back straight and both legs extended to the side in a V, feet flexed. Place the arms to the side of the body and rotate the spine to face the extended leg. Reach for the foot of the extended leg without lifting the opposite hip off the floor. Hinge at the hip with the back straight and then release the stretch to let the forehead relax on the knee. Exhale during the release. Come upright, facing the leg, and place the arms to the side of the body. Rotate to face front and repeat to the other side.

11. Quadriceps

Lie on one side and extend the bottom arm to support the head. Flex the knees in front of the body and point the feet, keeping them in line with the torso. With the top arm, take hold of the top ankle and pull the foot toward the buttock. Use an abdominal contraction to keep the lower back from arching. Inhale and then deepen the stretch during the exhale. Repeat three times and then repeat with the other leg.

12. Feet

Lie on the floor with the feet flat and the knees bent. Keeping the hips even, bring one knee toward the chest until the thigh is perpendicular to the floor. (See # 9). Flex and then circle the foot at the ankle five times, first in one direction and then the other. Repeat with the other foot.

When exercises are repeated over and over again, there is a tendency for students and teachers alike to become careless. Stay focused on what needs to be done. If you are very careful about how your students use their bodies, they will one day, also be as careful. If you expect a lot from them, they will expect a lot from themselves. If you are pleased with their success, they will be, too.

Turning and inclining the head

While lifting the head up and down, turning the head right and left, and tilting the head from side to side are ordinary, everyday movements, turning and inclining the head at the same time is not that common. Because it is an unusual position and because it is an integral part of artistic expression, give it special attention.

As you demonstrate the turned/inclined position, ask the class to imitate you. Remind the students to lift the chin slightly to produce the elegant, regal look

characteristic of the classical ballet dancer. To help students shape the position of the head correctly, use the image of a man shaving his cheek. Pretend to feel the sun shining on the side of the face. If imitation and images fail, use your hands to shape the position.

Neither action should dominate the other. If the head turns too far, the appearance of an unsightly muscle, called the sternocliedo-mastsoid, will protrude along one side of the neck. To minimize the turn, see both eyes in the mirror. If the head tilts too far, one side of the neck will look shorter than the other. Pretend to balance a bottle on top of the head. The inclination is deemed sufficient when the bottle falls off.

Once the students are able to turn and incline the head to both the right and to the left, practice circling the head down and around from one position to the other. For future reference, specify three signposts along this pathway—A (turned and inclined to the right), B (chin over the mid-line), and C (turned and inclined to left).

Begin sitting cross-legged on the floor, hands on the knees, head erect. Use a triple-meter. Turn and incline the head to the right, A (1-&-a)/circle the head until the chin reaches the mid-line, B (2-&-a)/turn and incline the head to the left, C (3-&-a)/bring the head erect (4-&-a). Reverse and repeat all.

Low, middle, and high fifth position of the arms

The three variations of fifth position of the arms are described in French as en bas (low), en avant (front or middle), and en haut (high). Use the mirror to study the lines of each position both from the front and from the side.

Correct

Correct

Incorrect

Incorrect

Create the oval shape of both high fifth and low fifth by drawing two perfect curves, free of any angles. Rotate the upper arms out and turn the hands in so that the palms of the hands and the insides of the elbows fall on the same plane. Open up the space between the wrists and the hands to lengthen the curve and cup the hands slightly, bringing the little fingers toward the body, to taper the curve. Keeping a space between the ends of the fingers, reach toward a point in space where both curves will eventually meet. Notice how aesthetics and technique support each other. Rotating the upper arms and lengthening the curves not only create beautiful lines but, at the same time, activate muscles that help the body to both balance and resist gravity.

In high fifth, hold the arms in front of the head so that the palms can be seen when looking up with the eyes only. Keep the shoulders lowered. Together, the side of the neck, the shoulder, and inside of the upper arm should draw the shape of a U.

In low fifth, hold the arms away from the body. Use the image of wearing heavy gold rings to help lengthen the arms and pull the shoulders down.

Shape middle fifth much the same way as low and high fifth. Rotate the upper arms without lifting the shoulders, turn the hands, bringing the little fingers closer to the body, and lengthen the fingers towards a point on the circle beyond the fingertips. Increase the bend of the elbows slightly to change the oval into a circle and place the elbows lower than the shoulders and the hands lower than the elbows in order to lead the eye of the observer to the face.

Once the three variations of fifth have been learned, link them together.

Begin in first position with the arms in low fifth. Use a slow triple-meter. Lift the arms to middle fifth (1-&-a)/ high fifth (2-&-a)/middle fifth (3-&-a)/low fifth (4)/battement tendu à la seconde with the right leg (&-a-5-&)/first position (a-6)/repeat (&-a-7-&)/(a-8). Repeat, executing the battement tendu with the left leg.

Second position of the arms

To shape second position, move one arm from high fifth to the side of the body. Maintain the shape of the arm, making sure that the inside of the palm and the inside of the elbow remain on the same plane. Work, facing the mirror.

To help maintain the rotation of the upper arm, feel as if the elbow is suspended by a string. At the same time, resist the rotation of the upper arm, by pulling the shoulder down. An intense stretch is usually felt through the back of the arm and on top of the elbow when the upper and lower arms rotate in opposite directions. This discomfort eases, however, once the arms become accustomed to the position.

Again, allow the curve of the arm to slope gently downward, elbow below shoulder and hand below elbow so that the line of the arm leads to the face. Rest the thumb, tension-free, in front of the fingers and separate the pointer as a way to taper the end of the curve.

The forearm and hand should be held without tension. These are the parts of the arm that will be used one day to make a gesture or accent a note of the music. It is difficult to see muscles gripping, but easy to feel. Test for tension by placing your hand on the top of a student's forearm.

Lengthen the curve by pulling the arm away from the center of the back. When the second arm is added, lengthen that curve in the opposite direction with equal energy. Think of a triangle, drawn across the back from elbow to elbow and from both elbows to the top of an elongated spine, suspending the body like a coat on a coat hanger, hanging from a rack. Notice how both arms lie on the circumference of a very, very big circle when they shape second position.

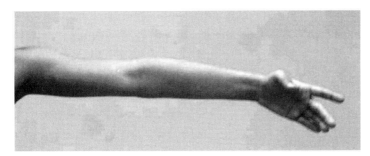

Correct

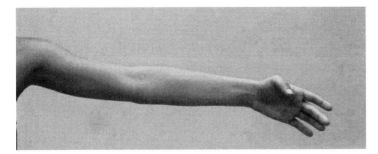

Incorrect

Port de bras, moving from low fifth, to middle fifth, to second position, and back to low fifth

Initiate the port de bras from low fifth to middle fifth by lifting low fifth to a point midway between the waist and the shoulder and bending the elbows a little to change the oval into a circle. Reach within the circumference of the circle without letting the fingers touch.

To open the arms from middle fifth to second position, lead with the forearms as if pushing curtains aside. At the same time, open the upper arms slightly from the shoulders to expand the position.

Since the oval of low fifth exists in second position, no adjustments are necessary as the arms return to low fifth. Simply lower the arms from the shoulders to surround a big egg.

Begin in first position with the arms in low fifth. Use a slow triple-meter. Lift the arms to middle fifth (a-1-&)/open to second position (a-2-&)/ return to low fifth (a-3-&)/hold (a-4-&). Repeat 4 times.

Transitioning the arms through second position to low fifth

As your students progress, a more complex, interesting, and expressive way to make the transition from second to low fifth may be used.

Place one arm in second position and initiate the movement of the arm by breathing in the scent of a beautiful rose. Turn the palm over and, without locking the elbow, open the wrist, lengthen the fingers, and reach toward the opposite wall. The arm will lift somewhat, not purposefully, but in response to the breath.

To lower the arm, replicate the descending action of the wave described earlier. Exhale and bend the elbow, shaping a perfect curve with the inside of the elbow facing up and the palm facing down. Let the arm float down gently to fold into low fifth. Remember to "pet the kitty," by lengthening the fingers at the end of the curve.

Practice the following exercise first with one arm and then with both arms. Notice when two arms transition from second position to low fifth, they move through the shape of a cereal bowl.

Begin in first position with the arms in low fifth. Use a triple-meter. Lift the arms to middle fifth (1-&-a, 2-&-a)/open to second position (3-&-a, 4-&-a)/ breath and reach (5-&-a)/bend elbows (6-&-a)/ lower the arms (7-&-a)/fold the lower arms into the curves of low fifth (8-&-a). Repeat 4 times.

When the class is able to use the hands and fingers correctly, during the transition through second position, execute the port de bras using fewer counts.

> Begin in first position with the arms in low fifth. Use a slow triple-meter. Lift the arms to middle fifth (1-&-a)/open to second position (2-&)/transition through second position (a)/elbows (3-&-a)/low fifth (4). Repeat 4 times.

Use the above port de bras during a grand plié exercise at the barre, but do not use it with a grand plié as yet.

First, second, and third arabesque à terre

When you introduce these three variations of the arabesque, explain the history of the word, arabesque, and show the class an example of the ancient geometric design for which it is named. Because beginning students are not yet ready to handle the physical demands of an arabesque en l'air, practice à terre, without music, and facing diagonally to the mirror. Name recognition is the primary goal of the first year. Begin to refine the shape of each position during the second year.

Describe the three arabesque positions using the French terms ouverte, en epaulée, and a deux bras or number them according to the Cecchetti method, first, second and third. To avoid confusion, use either the terms or numbers during the first year. As you move forward into the second year be ready to explain why some steps have more than one name or number and how various schools and teachers throughout Europe influenced the development of ballet vocabulary.

4 Transition steps

Transition steps can be used to cover space, shift weight from one foot to another, change direction within a combination, or provide momentum for a jump. Dynamically, they are often the calm before the storm.

Glissade derrière

Before this step is introduced, the class should be performing some exercises at the barre from fifth position and know how to execute a battement soutenu à la seconde. The following exercise may be practiced in anticipation of a glissade.

> Begin in fifth position with the right foot back, arms in low fifth. Use a slow triple-meter. Demi-plié (1-&)/battement tendu à la seconde en fondu, using the right leg (a-2-&)/demi-plié fifth position, right foot back (a-3-&) straighten (a-4). Repeat 4 times to the same side.

To execute a glissade derrière, begin in fifth position with the right foot back, arms in low fifth or middle third. Place the weight of the body over the front foot and keep it there during the demi-plié and as the right leg extends à la seconde. Push off the ball of the supporting foot, travelling through a low arc. Land on the right foot en fondu and slice the left foot into demi-plié fifth position front.

If the glissade travels in the direction of the back foot, and the back foot stays in back, it is said to be derrière. If it travels in the direction of the front foot and the front foot stays in front, it is described as devant.

Use the rotation of the legs to determine the angle of the feet in the V-shape of fifth position. Use the angle of the working foot to determine the direction of the glissade.

Carry the torso through space on top of the pelvis. Keep the flowerpot upright to prevent the torso from leaning to or away from the direction of the glissade. At the top of the glissade, bring the back leg opposite the front leg, heel in front of foot.

When the class is able to shape each part of the glissade correctly, perform the following sequence.

> Begin in fifth position with the right foot back, arms in low fifth or middle third. Use a duple-meter. Demi-plié (1)/glissade derrière (&-2)/straighten (3)/hold (4). Continue across the floor.

In order to repeat the above combination, transfer the weight of the body onto the ball of the front foot as the knees straighten following the final demi-plié.

Even though a glissade is not a jump, it requires enough thrust to draw the same shape that is seen at the top of all jumps, an upside down V, drawn when both knees straighten at the same time. Young dancers usually do not have the strength or coordination to achieve the elevation necessary to create this shape, but they should know what to work towards.

> Begin in fifth position with the right foot back, arms in low fifth or middle third. Use a duple-meter. Battement tendu à la seconde with the right leg (&-1)/fifth front (&-2)/battement tendu à la seconde right (&-3)/fifth back (&-4)/demi-plié (5)/glissade derrière (&-6)/ straighten (7)/hold (8). Repeat 4 times to the same side.

Use the glissade in an adage.

> Begin in fifth position with the right foot front, arms in low fifth. Use a slow triple-meter. Prepare the arms to second position through middle fifth on the last two counts of the preparation. Battement tendu à la seconde (&-a-1-&)/dégagé en l'air (a-2-&)/battement tendu à la seconde (a-3)/fifth position back (a-4)/demi-plié (5-&)/glissade derrière (a-6)/straighten (a-7)/hold (&-a-8). Repeat to the other side. Repeat all.

Glissade devant

Execute a glissade devant in the same way as a glissade derrière, but this time travel to the side in the direction of the front foot and finish the glissade with the same foot in front.

As the back leg pushes away from the floor, move it à la seconde to line up with the right leg at the peak of the glissade before it returns to fifth back.

Use the same combinations listed in the section above, substituting glissade devant for glissade derrière.

Sometimes, it is possible to pull a step from your students with little or no breakdown. Presenting an image or simply asking your students to imitate you without any preliminary discussion will produce the desired results. For instance, give the meaning of the word "glissade," show the step, explain that the step starts and finishes in fifth position, and then, without further ado, invite the class to pretend to be cats catching mice. With everyone in fifth position, hands held in front of the chest like paws, instruct the children to demi-plié, pounce on the mouse, straighten the knees, and wait one count. As the students pounce, add a sound effect such as ah-ha. Glissade might not look great for a while, but the class will grasp the essence of the step and have some fun as well.

5 PETITE ALLEGRO

Petite allegro is the culmination of all the fundamentals of basic ballet technique. Except for the shape of an arm or a position of a leg, the same principles of alignment, coordination, line, balance and musicality that have guided each step learned so far now guide the body as it goes into the air and returns to earth.

Sauté in first position

The sauté from first position can be introduced once students understand how to balance on the balls of the feet and are strong enough to rise to demi-pointe. Jumping from first is a natural extension of the relevé. It involves the same interaction of foot and floor, only the body is moved farther up into space before descending to the demi-plié. The muscles surrounding the hips, knees and feet play an important role in the ascent and descent of a jump, but the feet, because they are the last part of the body to leave and return to the floor, are paramount. They are responsible for the height, direction, shape, and musicality of the jump as well as a secure and noise-free landing.

Begin with the weight of the body over the balls of the feet in the starting position and keep the weight over the balls of the feet during the demi-plié that precedes the jump. At the end of the jump, land lightly, absorbing the weight through the balls of the feet so the heels may be lowered slowly and with control. Be sneaky when you come down. Say shhhhhh to the heels.

Reach the basement at the bottom of the demi-plié both before and after the jump. Shape a wide diamond with the knees over toes. At the top of the jump, do not open the legs wide but reach toward the floor with well-shaped feet.

Keep the body vertical during the preparation and the landing by hinging at the knees, not at the hips. Use the C-curve to maintain verticality in the air. Practically speaking, a vertical stance develops strength in the legs and feet. Aesthetically, it makes jumping look effortless.

To help keep the body upright, think of balancing a book on top of the head. Introduce "George" to the class, an imaginary helper. Place him on the sternum and take care not to let poor George fall off! To help maintain the length of the arms and to prevent them from bouncing, use the image of wearing heavy gold rings.

To avoid losing momentum, do not sit in the basement of the demi-plié but move through it to jump. Make a sound effect such as daaaaayump to emphasize the connection between the down and the up. Even if the dancers must work half-time, choose music that supports jumping, that is lively with lots of notes. The tracks on CDs, labeled battement tendu or battement dégagé, usually work well. A tarantella actually sounds like a bouncing ball.

Some instructors first practice a jump at the barre. This can be useful when studying the shape of the legs in the air but bring the jump to the center as soon as possible so that the dancers do not come to rely more on the barre than the legs for elevation.

Begin in first position with the arms in low fifth. Use a quick duple-meter. Demi-plié (1)/sauté (2)/demi-plié first position (3)/straighten knees (4). Repeat 4 times.

Begin in first position with the arms in low fifth. Use a quick duple-meter. Demi-plié (1)/sauté (&)/demi-plié first position (2) straighten (3)/hold (4). Repeat 8 times.

Changement de pieds

At the top of a changement, the foot that begins fifth position front passes by the back leg, shaping a narrow V before finishing fifth position back. The legs open at the top of the jump, not purposefully, but as a result of the feet pushing away from the floor. If necessary, lie on the floor to practice how the legs and feet stretch at the top of the changement.

Begin in fifth position with the right foot in front, arms in low fifth. Use a duple-meter. Demi-plié (1)/changement (&-2)/straighten (3)/hold (4). Repeat left foot front. Repeat all 4 times.

Begin in fifth position with the right foot front, arms in low fifth. Use a duple-meter. Demi-plié (1)/changement 2 times (&-2,&-3)/straighten (4). Repeat 4 times.

Begin in fifth position with the left foot front, arms in low fifth. Use a duple-meter. Demi-plié (1)/glissade derrière (&-2)/changement (&-3)/straighten (4). Repeat to the other side. Repeat all.

During the glissade in the above combination, the pulse before the count (&) indicates the moment when the right foot touches down, and the count (2) refers to the left foot closing fifth. During the changement, the pulse before the count (&) indicates the jump, and the count (3) refers to the landing.

Begin in fifth position with the left foot front, arms in low fifth. Use a duple-meter. Demi-plié on the last count of the preparation. Glissade derrière (&-1)/ changement (&-2)/glissade derrière (&-3)/changement (&-4)/glissade derrière (&-5)/ changement 3 times (&-6)/(&-7)/(&-8). Repeat to the other side.

As you teach the petite and grand allegro, the top of a jump, the picture formed in the air, with few exceptions, is a V, shaped by the legs and feet. The V-shape may be wide or narrow, even off center, but it exists in everything from a changement, to a glissade, a jeté, a sissonne, an embôité, a grand jeté, a saut de basque, and even a tour jeté. Set this goal for your students long before they can accomplish it. Encourage them to use the floor and jump with full energy to lift the hips off the floor high enough for the legs to extend fully. Only by making an effort will a dancer grow stronger.

Vocalize both the counts and the pulses to help beginning students connect rhythm to movement. As the class advances, however, know that it is not necessary to vocalize every count and every pulse of every step, only those that need emphasis.

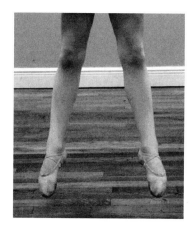

Échappé sauté

The position of an échappé sauté in the air varies according to the style of teaching. One method may call for fifth position en l'air before landing in second and before returning to fifth. This is a good preparation for échappé battu. Another method may call for second position en l'air at the top of the first jump and fifth position en l'air on the return. Shaping the legs in a V on the way out and on the way in is also acceptable. Note that all three share the same objective, to jump high and stretch the feet and legs.

> Begin in fifth position with the right foot front, arms in low fifth. Use a duple-meter. Demi-plié (1)/échappé to second position demi-plié (&-2)/sauté to fifth position demi-plié, right foot back (&-3)/straighten (4). Repeat left foot front. Repeat all.

The two jumps that are part of an echappé sauté should be equal in height. Sometimes dancers make less of an effort during the second jump. While the feet open just beyond the shoulders, emphasize height, not width.

> Begin in fifth position with the right foot front, arms in low fifth. Use a duple-meter. Demi-plié on the last count of the preparation. Changement (&-1)/changement (&-2)/échappé to second position demi-plié (&-3)/ sauté to fifth position demi-plié, right foot back (&-4). Repeat left foot front. Repeat all.

> Begin in fifth position with the left foot front, arms in low fifth. Use a duple-meter. Demi-plié on the last count of the preparation. Glissade derrière to the right (&-1)/échappé to second position demi-plié (&-2)/sauté to fifth position demi-plié, right foot front (&-3)/glissade derrière to the left (&-4). Repeat to the other side. Repeat all.

The above exercise combines a step that travels with one that moves straight up and down. Make sure that all contrasting directional changes are clearly defined and that the distribution of weight at the end of one movement prepares for the movement that follows.

Assemblé dessus

The word, "assemblé," describes how the supporting leg and the working leg come together in the air at the top of the jump. Because beginning students rarely have the strength and coordination to get up high enough to accomplish this feat, expect them only to point their feet in the air and land, touching both heels to the floor at the same time. They should be aware how to perform the step correctly, however, so that they know what goal to work towards.

Dessus, meaning over, describes the path taken by the working leg as it returns

Some steps both travel and go up, drawing an arc in the air. The arc may be wide and flat, like an upside down grin, narrow and high like an upside down U, or as long and as high as the path of an arrow. For example, the path of a glissade is low to the ground, just high enough to point the feet. The emphasis is on the distance traveled. Steps such as pas de chat and brisé go up as much or more than they travel. In a grand jeté both the height of the jump and the space covered are equal.

to fifth position. While the working leg, the leg that brushes off the floor, may begin in fifth position back or front, it must finish fifth position front, over and on top of the supporting leg, the leg that pushes off the floor.

Place the weight over the ball of the supporting foot in the starting fifth. Begin to slide the working leg out of fifth position back (or front) and just as the ball of the foot brushes off of the floor, push straight up in the air from the ball of the supporting foot. Make sure that the working foot moves in the direction of the toes with the heel in front of the foot. As the working leg separates from the supporting leg, keep the hips square, headlights aimed to the front. Land softly.

> Begin in fifth position with the right foot in back, arms in low fifth. Use a duple-meter. Demi-plié (1)/assemblé dessus (&–2)/straighten (3)/hold (4). Repeat left foot back. Repeat all.

> Begin in fifth position with the right foot in back, arms in low fifth. Use a duple-meter. Demi-plié (1)/glissade (&–2)/assemblé dessus (&–3)/straighten (4). Repeat to the other side. Repeat all.

Soubresaut

Before attempting the soubresaut, show the class how to shape a pointed fifth position en l'air. Sit on the floor with the legs extended to the front and shape one foot with two heels, a soussus but with the toes extended. With a straight back, lean back slightly, supporting the weight of the torso on both hands, and lift the legs a few inches. Tap the legs together a few times to develop a sense of where the legs make contact. Call the point of contact, the "kissing spot." Next, try with the other leg on top. Note that this position lays the foundation for batterie.

> Begin in fifth position with the right foot in front, arms in low fifth. Use a quick duple-meter. Demi-plié (1)/soubresaut (&)/demi-plié fifth position, right foot front (2)/straighten (3)/hold (4). Repeat 4 times.

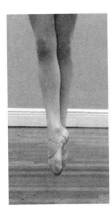

Begin in fifth position with the right foot in front, arms in low fifth. Use a duple-meter. Demi-plié (1)/soubresaut (&-2)/changement (&-3)/straighten (4). Repeat left foot front. Repeat all.

Begin in fifth position with the right foot in back, arms in low fifth. Use a duple-meter. Demi-plié (1)/assemblé dessus (&-2)/soubresaut (&-3)/straighten (4). Repeat left foot back. Repeat all.

Sissonne fermé de côté dessus

A sissonne is sometimes called the scissors step because of the rapid action of opening and closing the legs, like two blades of a scissors cutting the air. No matter what the direction, a sissonne always jumps from two feet and finishes on one.

De côté indicates that the step travels sideways and fermée indicates that the second leg closes in fifth position as opposed to remaining en l'air. Whether the second leg begins in fifth back or front, if it passes over the supporting leg to finish in front, it is said to be dessus.

Begin the step in fifth position with the right foot in front, arms in low fifth. Execute a demi-plié and spring up and to the side. To prevent the body from tilting in the direction of the jump, keep the flowerpot on the table.

Open the legs at the same time and with equal energy. Rotate the leg that begins in fifth position back to bring it even with the other leg, heel in front of foot and make sure that the distance traveled equals the height of the jump.

Land on the right foot and immediately slide the left foot into fifth position front. Changing legs at the end of the sissonne is not required, but it feels more organic. Make sure that the front foot crosses in fifth position so that the balls of the feet are close to center and ready to move the body. Note that crossing the feet is not unduly stressful when the knees are bent but remember that a crossed fifth does not necessarily mean a tight fifth.

THE END OF CLASS  6

The exercises given at the end of class should be upbeat and leave the students with a feeling of exhilaration. Remember that class work is intense and sometimes frustrating. Children need a release after such demanding work and, don't forget, having some fun will bring them back to you yet another day.

All of the exercises listed below begin in the upstage corner, travel downstage on a diagonal, and are performed by the dancers, one or two at a time. Teach the students how to line up, walk into place, take a preparatory position, and watch and listen for the musical cue that tells them when to begin. This ritual helps develop spatial and rhythmic awareness.

Triplets

A triplet is a set of three steps, one step en fondu and two on demi-pointe, executed with the legs parallel. Triplets develop rhythmic skills and prepare for pas de bourrée and balancé depending on how the three steps are combined. In preparation for the pas de bourrèe, the pattern of down-up-up, down-up-up or up-up-down, up-up-down may be used. A more complex variation echoes the rhythm of a balancé, down-up-down, down-up-down. Master one pattern before introducing a new one.

Start in the upstage left corner and, facing the downstage right corner, extend the right leg pointe tendue. Place the hands on the shoulders, and later, in second position, once that position has been mastered.

Use a Mazurka or clap your hands to indicate the rhythm of the steps. Let six counts go by to allow the first person in line to move into place and take her position. During the second count of six, when the first girl begins her series of triplets traveling downstage, signal the next student to step up and prepare to go. Once everyone has a turn, repeat the series starting from the opposite corner.

As you begin to use the words upstage and downstage, tell the class how the words came to be used. Explain that a stage was once built on a slant so that the audience, sitting on a level surface, could see the performer from head to toe. The words "upstage" and "downstage" were used to indicate where to stand and which way to go on the slanted stage. Today, the audience sits on a slant and the stage is level.

Pony steps

Pony steps are small jumps changing from one foot to another as the working knee lifts in front of the body in a low turned-in attitude. These jumps prepare for embôité. They can be done in place or move downstage as well as travel from corner to corner.

Begin the step standing with the feet parallel and the hands on the hips. Make sure the supporting foot points as it shifts a vertical torso up and onto the other leg. Like the step, the tempo of the music should be light and lively.

Chassé

A series of chassés allows beginning students to experience the joy of jumping and moving through space. Refinement of the step will come eventually, but during the first year the emphasis is on fun, not form.

Teach the chassé through the demonstration/imitation technique. Name it, do it, and invite your students to follow. Give the class the rhythm of the step using the words slide, together, slide, together, slide, together.

Start in the upstage left corner. Stand in fifth position with the right foot in front and face the downstage right corner. Execute the chassé moving diagonally downstage, one student at a time. Allow four counts per student. When music is added, use a fast triple-meter.

To help the class understand the depth of the slide, use the image of a snow-plow. To help students shape fifth position en l'air, remind them of the kissing spot.

Do not confuse a chassé with a gallop. Both are rhythmically alike, but the gallop uses the step-together means of propulsion, whereas the chassé uses the slide-together form. To avoid confusion, concentrate only on the chassé. As a linking step, it is more useful to beginning students.

Mud-puddle/grand jeté

Place any object in the center of the room to represent a mud puddle. Line up the children in the upstage corner and invite each one to run to the center and fly over the puddle. Play lively, energetic music that echoes running and jumping. Children never tire of the game that foreshadows the grand jeté.

Chaînés turns

Chaînés turns introduce the concept of spotting, challenging the dancer to control the body as it spins through space. Executing these turns properly is far beyond the level of first year students, but they will have a lot of fun trying to do them.

First, wow your class with a demonstration of the real thing, fast and furious chaînés from corner to corner. Your class will be dazzled. When they recover, break the step down. Start in the upstage left corner, and, facing left, pointe tendue quatrième devant with the right leg. Place the hands on the shoulder with the elbows pointed to the side. Step onto the diagonal with the right foot and pivot a half-turn to step on the diagonal with the left foot. Continue diagonally downstage, stepping right, then left, then right, etc., making sure the elbows remain wide. Most beginners cannot sustain demi-pointe during a series of turns, but encourage them to try.

Designate an object in the downstage corner as a focal point. Explain how "spotting" helps dancers to turn in a straight line and lessens the dizzying effects of spinning fast.

You can use music, but don't expect the step to be rhythmical. Calling out right, left, right, left to direct the feet will be more useful. Practice one at a time, allowing each student eight counts to prepare and eight counts to execute the series of turns.

Révérance

Performing a révérance, given at the very end of class, brings the children back down to earth. Performing a simple port de bras or a curtsy, applauding, or shaking your hand are different ways to show appreciation for the class. Whatever ritual you choose, take it seriously and use it consistently.

Part II
Elementary 2: Syllabus for the Second Year

You will find that moving from the first year to the second is not as simple as turning the page of a book. The class may need more work in a certain area or perhaps they have already jumped ahead. So much depends on the amount of time spent with the class and the level of motivation and talent. Follow your instincts.

Barre exercises

Demi plié in fourth position
Grand plié, using the arm and head
Grand plié in positions four and five
Battement tendu, using the arm and the head
Battement dégagé quatrième devant and derrière
Battement piqué
Rond de jambe à terre in two counts
Battement frappé single en croix and double à la seconde
Battement retiré derrière from fifth position back
Battement passé
Dégagé en l'air en fondu
Demi-grand rond de jambe en l'air
Attitude en l'air devant and derrière
Rond de jambe en l'air
Battement fondu sur le cou-de-pied devant and derrière
Extending attitude en l'air from battement fondu sur le cou-de-pied
Grand battement en croix
Piqué to fifth position and to retiré derrière
Relevé sur le cou-de-pied, battement relevé retiré, and battement relevé passé
Cambré side, front, and back

Center exercises:

Body positions
Glissade changée
Glissade en avant
Pas de bourrée dessous
Sissonne simple
Pas de chat
Échappé sauté with port de bras
Jeté dessus
Pirouette en dehors

AT THE BARRE

Beginning and ending an exercise

Continue to remind students to prepare for the preparation of an exercise as if they were in the wings, waiting to make an entrance or posed on stage ready to perform—mind alert, body balanced, center strong, legs rotated, and head and arms shaped properly.

There is no rule dictating how the head should be held at the start and finish of an exercise. The position, however, should be appropriate to the level of the student and used consistently. I prefer that students study how to turn and incline the head during the first year, but that they hold the head erect when they work so that they can concentrate on the alignment of the body and the shape of the legs and feet. By the second year, however, they should start and finish an exercise with the arm in low fifth and the head turned and inclined away from the barre, eyes focused in the direction of the nose.

If an exercise ends in a demi-plié fifth position, encourage students to evaluate both the depth and alignment of the position before the knees straighten and the head turns and inclines. If an exercise ends with the arm in second position, expect students to return the arm to low fifth, turning and inclining the head as the hand folds in to complete the curve. Continue to remind students to hold the final pose for a moment.

Preparation of the arm to second position, using the head

For most of the first year of training, the working arm is held in low or middle fifth at the barre. Toward the end of the first year, after learning to prepare the arm

to second position, the arm is held to the side of the body during some exercises, for example grand battement à la seconde, to keep it out of the way of the working leg. During the second year, a preparation of the arm to second position is performed before most exercises along with coordinating head movements.

Prepare for the preparation by standing in fifth position with the arm in low fifth, the head turned and inclined away from the barre (position A), eyes focused in the direction of the nose. Use the first two counts of a four-count preparation (triple-meter) as a call to action.

Lift the arm to middle fifth on the pulse (a) before the count (3), turning and inclining the top of the head toward the barre (position C) and looking into the palm of the hand as if reading a secret message written there. Be careful that the focus of the eyes does not pull the chin down or prevent the head from turning and inclining sufficiently. On the final count (4), open the arm to second position and turn and incline the head away from the barre (position A), eyes focused in the direction of the nose. Again, make sure the height of the chin and the incline of the head are not affected when the head shifts from one side to the other.

On the first count of the exercise following the preparation, bring the head erect and focus the eyes front.

Grand plié, using the arm and head

First study the path of the head during a grand plié. Begin with the head turned and inclined away from the barre (position A), circle the head until the chin is over the mid-line but without touching the chest (position B), circle the head until it reaches a turned and inclined position toward the barre (position C, the direct opposite of A), and finally shift the head back to the starting position, turned and inclined away from the barre (position A). Notice that the nose draws a half-circle moving from A to C and that the eyes follow the nose.

Once the path of the head is understood, match the head positions to the four parts of the grand plié. Start in first position with the head in position A, begin to circle the head as the knees bend, reach position B at the bottom of the grand plié, circle to position C as the heels touch the floor, and shift back to position A as the knees straighten.

Position A

Position B

&-a

Next, examine how the arm works with the head. Prepare the arm to second position through middle fifth, looking into the palm as the head inclines to (position C) and then away from the barre (position A). Instead of pausing in second position, move through it on the two pulses (&-a) following the last count (4) of the preparation. Inhale to turn the palm and extend through the fingers. Make sure the breath lifts the face and opens the chest.

On the first count following the preparation, release the breath and bend the elbow as the head circles to the outside of the body. On the second count, complete the shape of low fifth as the head reaches position B, chin over the mid-line, eyes focused into the palm. On the count of three, lift the arm to middle fifth as the head circles to position C, turned and inclined to the barre, chin lifted, eyes focused into the palm. On the count of four, open the arm to second, following the hand with the head until the head reaches position A, turned and inclined away from the barre.

When the arm and head are able to move through each position together, clearly and smoothly, add the positions of the head and arm to the grand plié.

1   *2*   *3*

Begin in first position with the arm in low fifth. Use a slow triple-meter. Demi-plié (1-&)/straighten (a-2)/middle fifth (3-&)/second position (a-4)/extend the arm through second position (&-a)/grand plié, using the arm (5-8)/extend the arm through second position (&-a)/grand plié (1-4)/extend the arm through second position (&)/bend the elbow (a) low fifth (5)/battement tendu à la seconde (a-6) flat (a-7)/adjust inside leg toward barre (a-8).

Repeat the above combination in second position, adjusting the inside leg toward the body (6) so that it is ready to support the body during the battement tendu à la seconde (a-7) and as the leg returns from pointe tendue to first position (a-8).

Before a grand plié, remember to move the arm through second position without pausing so that the arm is able to lengthen through the fingers before the elbow bends. To begin the grand plié, bend the elbow and the knees at the same time.

In the ascending demi-plié, incline the head to the barre from the neck, not the waist. Keep the torso (cereal box) erect and be careful not to let the fingers of the working hand cross the mid-line.

Coordinating all the movements that accompany a grand plié is an ongoing challenge. Do not hesitate to break the step down for review whenever you notice a student losing form.

Grand plié in fourth and fifth positions

Because fourth and fifth positions are considered stressful on the knees, many teachers have eliminated them from the barre. Instead of giving them up, I began to use them sparingly, beginning the class with grand pliés in first and second positions, and then, further into the barre, adding a grand plié in fifth or fourth at the end of an exercise, along with a cambré and a balance on demi-pointe.

Ideally, the feet should run parallel to each other in fourth position, lined up heel to toe and toe to heel and separated by the distance of the length of the student's foot, measured between the toe of the back leg and the heel of the front leg, about six inches. If the student is unable to cross the feet in fourth, however, allow an open position where the heel of the working leg lines up with the middle of the standing foot, much like an open third position.

Make sure that rotation determines the angle of the feet so that the knees fall over the toes when they bend and remember to maintain the shape of the feet as the thighs open. Follow this same principle when teaching a grand plié in fifth position. Practice both steps facing the barre until the students are strong enough to sustain alignment during the plié.

 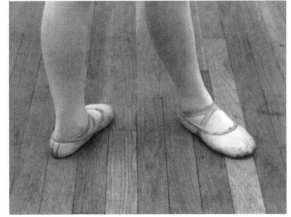

Battement dégagé quatrième devant and derrière

Battement dégagé is also called battement tendu jeté (Russian school) and battement glissé (French school). Begin with the battement dégagé quatrième devant and then add quatrième derrière when ready. Use the technical information and the images presented in the first level concerning battement tendu quatrième devant and derrière and battement dégagé à la seconde.

Pay special attention to dégagé quatrième derrière. This is the first time that the leg lifts off the floor to the back. If you put in the work on this position now, the arabesque en l'air will grow quite naturally from it. Make sure that rotation is maintained to and from fifth position, that the abdominal scoop supports the pelvis as the torso shifts forward, and that the spiral of the upper body responds to the rotation of the leg. Return to vertical when the back leg returns to fifth position, but note that once dégagé quatrième increases in speed and is executed in a series, the shift of the torso should be maintained until the series ends.

Battement piqué

A battement piqué follows from battement dégagé. During a battement piqué, the working leg extends, taps the floor lightly, rebounding off of it. After the rebound, the leg can close, pass through first position, or circle to another position.

By developing a strong connection between foot and ankle, battement piqué paves the way for a piqué to fifth position.

> Begin in first position with the arm in low fifth. Use a duple-meter. Battement dégagé à la seconde (&-1)/piqué (2)/first position (&-3)/ hold (4). Repeat 8 times.

For variety, execute the battement piqué, using the three count division of a Mazurka.

> Begin in first position with the arm in low fifth. Battement dégagé à la seconde (&-1)/piqué (2)/first position (&-3). Repeat 8 times.

In the exercises below, note that the working leg opens during each battement piqué on the pulse before the count. This timing lays the groundwork for a battement dégagé that opens on the pulse and closes on the count.

> Begin in first position with the arm in low fifth. Use a duple-meter. Battement dégagé à la seconde (&-1)/first position (&-2)/repeat three times (3-6)/battement dégagé à la seconde (&)/piqué (7)/first position (&-8). Repeat 4 times.

Begin in fifth position with the arm in low fifth. Use a duple-meter. Prepare the arm to second position through middle fifth. Battement dégagé quatrième devant (&-1)/fifth position (&-2)/battement dégagé à la seconde (&-3)/fifth position back (&-4)/battement dégagé quatrième derrière (&-5)/fifth position (&-6)/battement piqué à la seconde (&-7) fifth position back (&-8). Reverse and repeat all.

Begin in fifth position with the arm in low fifth. Use a duple-meter. Prepare the arm to second position through middle fifth. Battement piqué quatrième devant (&-1)/fifth position (&-2)/battement piqué à la seconde (&-3)/fifth position back (&-4)/battement piqué quatrième derrière (&-5)/brush through first position to quatrième devant (&-6)/through first position to quatrième derrière (&-7)/fifth position (&-8). Reverse and repeat all.

Rond de jambe à terre in two counts

When a student is given only two counts to complete the half-circle of the rond de jambe à terre, care must be taken to maintain turnout and resistance, especially as the leg moves quatrième derrière.

Begin in fifth position with the arm in low fifth. Use a slow triple-meter. Prepare the arm to second position through middle fifth. Battement tendu quatrième devant (a-1-&)/rond de jambe en dehors (a-2-&)/through first position to tendu quatrième devant (a-3-&)/ rond de jambe en dehors (a-4-&)/through first position to tendu quatrième devant (a-5-&)/degage en l'air (a-6-&)/through first to tendu quatrième derrière (a-7-&)/fifth position (a-8). Reverse and repeat all.

When the working leg reaches a position on the count and has time to spare during the following pulse, do not rest. Instead, keep the position alive by maximizing the stretch, the rotation, and the resistance needed to balance both.

Whether the foot moves out of fifth, into fifth, or through first position determines where the working foot points on the floor in relationship to the standing foot. Moving out of fifth, the toes travel in a straight line from the standing heel. Moving out of first, the heel travels in a straight line from the standing heel. If the working leg is about to move through first position from pointe tendue quatrième derrière, the pointed foot stays to the outside of the standing leg to allow room for the working heel to come through first position. If the working leg is about to close in fifth from pointe tendue quatrième derrière, then the toes of the working leg line up with the heel of the supporting leg before moving into the fifth.

In the first year, during the execution of a battement tendu, it was necessary to vocalize two pulses and a count to remind students to lift the heel and slide the ball of the foot, to stretch the top of the ankle, and to lengthen the toes. By the second year, students should be able to slide the ball of the foot and stretch the top of the ankle on the pulse (a) shape the tendu on the count (1) and further extend the leg from the hip on the following pulse (&).

Battement frappé quatrième devant

The placement of the working foot in preparation for battement frappé quatrième devant is the same as the one used for battement frappé à la seconde.

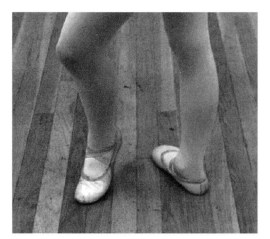

The foot is flexed without tension, lightly touching in front of the supporting ankle. The thigh is open and the knee is aligned with the toes.

Keeping the heel in front of the foot to maintain rotation, place the ball of the foot on the floor. Slide the pencil and, at the last minute, give it a shove, stretching the toes and the knee to fully extend the leg. Do not lift the leg up at the end of the frappé but direct the energy of the frappé into the floor.

To bring the foot back to its starting position, bend the knee, open the thigh, and pull the foot back to flex at the ankle.

Use a slow duple-meter to accompany a frappé exercise or increase the tempo and work half-time.

Begin in fifth position with the arm in low fifth. Prepare the arm to second position through middle fifth. Flex in front of the ankle (1)/battement frappé quatrième devant (&-2)/pointe tendu quatrième devant (3)/fifth position (&-4). Repeat 8 times.

Begin in fifth position with the arm in low fifth. Prepare the arm to second position through middle fifth. Flex in front of the ankle (1)/battement frappé quatrième devant (&-2)/flex in front of the ankle (3)/battement frappé à la seconde (&-4)/flex in front of the ankle (5)/battement frappé quatrième devant (&-6)/pointe tendue quatrième devant (7)/fifth position (&-8). Repeat 4 times.

Begin in fifth position with the arm in low fifth. Prepare the arm to second position through middle fifth. Flex in front of the ankle (1)/battement frappé quatrième devant (&-2)/battement piqué (3)/fifth position (&-4). Repeat à la seconde closing fifth position front. Repeat all 4 times.

Battement frappé quatrième derrière

Before teaching the battement frappé derrière, practice moving the working foot from fifth position back to a flexed position behind the ankle. Bend the working knee to allow the thigh to rotate and, at the same time, bring the inside of the ankle to the calf.

Rotate the top of the thigh to initiate the frappé. Once again, use the image of sliding and pushing a pencil. If the foot is shaped properly with the toes extending back from the heel, only the medial portion of the ball and big toe will make contact with the floor. Make sure the smiley face on the knee continues to face to the side as the leg extends.

As the working thigh pushes back and the knee begins to straighten, shift the torso forward and up. Allow the hip to open slightly in order to maintain the rotation of the leg. To resist these actions, scoop the abdominal muscles, hold the ribs together, stretch the working arm to the side from the middle of the back to keep the outside shoulder in place, and spiral the supporting side, from shoulder to ankle, in opposition to the force of the frappé.

Bend the knee to return the heel to the calf. Because rotation increases as the knee bends, the top of the leg should open out as the bottom half of the leg comes in. Bending the knee also signals the body to come upright. Note that the foot may skim the floor on the return, but it should not do so deliberately.

The class is ready to execute a battement frappé en croix once battement frappé quatrième derrière is mastered.

Begin in fifth position with the arm in low fifth. Use a slow duple-meter or work half-time to a quick duple. Prepare the arm to second position through middle fifth. Flex in front of the ankle (1)/battement frappé quatrième devant (&-2)/battement tendu quatrième devant (3)/fifth position (&-4). Repeat 4 times en croix.

Begin in fifth position with the arm in low fifth. Use a slow duple-meter or work half-time to a quick duple. Prepare the arm to second position through middle fifth. Flex in front of the ankle front (1)/frappé quatrième devant (&-2)/flex in front of the ankle (3)/frappé à la seconde (&-4)/ flex in back of the ankle (5)/frappé quatrième derrière (&-6)/ battement piqué (7)/fifth position (&-8). Reverse and repeat all.

Begin in fifth position with the arm in low fifth. Use a slow duple-meter or work half-time to a quick duple. Prepare the arm to second position through middle fifth. Flex in front of the ankle (1)/ frappé quatrième devant (&-2)/ flex in front of the ankle (3)/frappé à la seconde (&-4)/flex in back of the ankle (5)/frappé quatrième derrière (&-6)/brush through first position (7)/fifth position front (&-8). Repeat counts 1-6; battement piqué (7)/fifth position back (&-8). Reverse and repeat all.

Double frappé à la seconde

Begin the study of double frappé à la seconde by flexing the working foot and placing it in front of the supporting ankle. Flex without tension, keeping the angle between the ankle and the foot greater than ninety degrees.

With the hips square, open the working thigh to the side as far as it will go. Hold the barre lightly so that the supporting side, not the supporting hand, resists the action of the working thigh.

We say lead with the toes and come back with the heel when we want the leg to move to the back and return, just as we say lead with the heel and return with the toes when we want the leg to move to the front and return. These words can produce the required results, but make sure the class is clear about the mechanics. To begin any movement, the brain should hear the command, "rotate."

Maintain rotation during a double beat by moving the bottom half of the leg in and out, hinging at the knee. If the foot moves from the front to the back, rotation cannot be sustained. Tap the lower calf of the supporting leg with the inside of the heel and tap the front of the supporting ankle with the outside of the flexed foot. The heel of the beating foot should never hit the sensitive Achilles tendon.

Practice a series of beats before adding the frappé.

> Begin in first position with the arm in low fifth. Use a staccato duple-meter. Battement tendu à la seconde (&-1)/flex in front of the ankle (2)/flex in back of the ankle (3)/flex in front of the ankle (4)/flex in back of the ankle (5)/ flex in front of the ankle (6)/pointe tendue à la seconde (7)/first position (&-8)/ Reverse. Repeat all 4 times.

Except for the number of beats, execute the double frappé exactly like the single. From a flexed position, find the floor with the ball of the foot, slide it in the direction of the knee, and then brush off of the floor, pulling the bottom half of the working leg into a straight line and pointing the foot.

> Begin in first position with the arm in low fifth. Use a staccato duple-meter. Battement tendu à la seconde (&-1)/flex in front of the ankle (2)/flex in back of the ankle (3)/frappe à la seconde (4)/pointe tendue (5)/first position (&-6)/ demi-plié (7)/straighten (8). Reverse. Repeat all 4 times.

> Begin in first position with the arm in low fifth. Use a staccato duple-meter. Prepare the arm to second position through middle fifth. Battement tendu à la seconde (&-1)/beat front and back (2-&)/frappé à la seconde (3)/fifth position back (&-4). Reverse. Repeat all 8 times.

In the previous combination, the count and the following pulse (2-&) reflect the two beats of the frappé.

Moving the foot from fifth position back to point sur le cou-de-pied derrière

Moving from fifth position back to point sur le cou-de-pied derrière is much more complex than moving from fifth front, especially for beginning students. Because beginners usually lack the strength to fully rotate the legs when the legs are close together and the heels are on the floor, the feet and knees face diagonally front. Consequently, when the back knee bends, it runs into the supporting knee. When this traffic jam occurs, the students generally make one of two bad choices. They either bend the supporting knee to allow the back leg to pass or they sickle the back foot so that the working thigh has room to swing out and away from the standing leg. As a temporary fix, until the rotators strengthen, separate the back toes from the front heel, about an inch, so that the knee has room to bend. With the weight on the ball of the supporting foot, peel the working foot off the floor over the first three toes, stretching it diagonally toward the floor in line with the knee as the heel surrounds the calf.

To return the foot to the floor, separate the working calf from the ankle and fold the foot into the footprint of fifth position back.

To resist the rotating force of the working thigh, lengthen the body away from the working leg. Press through the ball of the supporting foot and, at the same time, scoop the abdominal muscles to deepen the C-curve.

Begin in fifth position with both hands on the barre. Use a slow duple-meter or work half-time to a quick duple. Lift back heel (1)/point en l'air (&)/sur le cou-de-pied derrière (2)/move the foot over the footprint (&)/toes/ball (3)/heel (4)/battement tendu à la seconde (&-5)/first position (&-6)/battement tendu à la seconde (&-7)/fifth position back (&-8). Repeat 4 times.

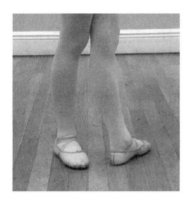

Correct

Correct

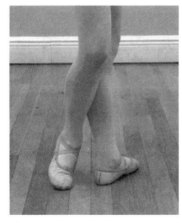

Correct

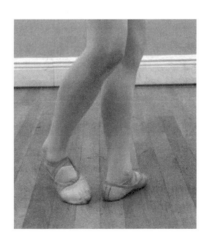

Incorrect

So that the working knee has space to lift when the above combination repeats, remember to keep a space between the toes and the supporting heel as the working leg closes fifth position back at the end of the second battement tendu à la seconde.

> Begin in fifth position with the arm in low fifth. Use a triple-meter. Prepare the arm to second position through middle fifth. Battement tendu quatrième devant (a-1-&)/rond de jambe en dehors (a-2-&)/through first to tendu quatrième devant (a-3-&)/rond de jambe en dehors (a-4-&)/sur le cou-de-pied derrière (a-5-&)/sur le cou-de-pied devant (a-6-&)/sur le cou-de-pied derrière (a-7)/move the foot over the footprint (&) toes/ball (a) heel (8). Reverse and repeat all.

> Begin in fifth position with the arm in low fifth. Use a duple-meter. Lift heel (&)/point en l'air (a)/sur le cou-de-pied devant (1)/sur le cou-de-pied derrière (&-2)/sur le cou-de-pied devant (&-3)/move the foot over the footprint (&) toes/ball (a)/heel (4)/ battement piqué quatrième devant (&-5)/fifth position (&-6)/battement piqué à la seconde (&-7)/fifth position back (&-8). Reverse and repeat all.

Battement retiré derrière

Once the students are able to move the foot from fifth position to point sur le cou-de-pied derrière, introduce battement retiré derrière. Slide the heel of the working foot up in a straight line behind the supporting leg until it reaches the back of the knee. Lift the foot as high as it can go without displacing the hips. Once the foot reaches the apex, only a tip of the inside of the heel should touch

the back of the knee. This shape will later define a piqué turn.

To return to fifth position, reverse the path of the foot to point sur le cou-de-pied derrière. From there, separate the foot from the calf and release it into the footprint of the starting fifth.

Battement passé

Knowing how to move the foot from fifth position to point in front and in back of the ankle, how to use the leg to move the foot from the front to the back and from the back to the front of the ankle, and how to shape the foot in front and in back of the knee are the prerequisite skills that prepare for battement passé. Transitioning from front to back and back to front at the knee are the only new elements to be learned.

  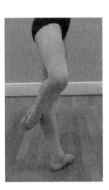

Begin in fifth position with the weight over the back foot. Lift the front foot to point sur le cou-de-pied devant and slide the little toenail up the leg. Just before reaching retiré devant, begin to lift the foot over an imaginary stick, extending perpendicular to the supporting leg. At the same time, open the thigh to pull the foot retiré derrière, inside of the working heel touching in back of the knee. Keep the hips square and the flowerpot on the table throughout.

Increasing the height of the working foot will one day be used to sustain balance at the end of a pirouette. The outward rotation of the thigh that moves the foot from the front of the knee to the back will help turn the body. As you introduce the battement passé, explore briefly the relationship of this step to a pirouette. As soon as you demonstrate a pirouette, your students will certainly try to imitate you because turning looks like so much fun. Remember that connecting what the class is working on now with what they will be working on in the future is a strong motivator.

Once the heel reaches retiré derrière, slide it down the back of the leg. To fold the foot into fifth position, separate the heel from the calf as the toes near the floor and roll through the foot. To prepare for a battement passé moving from fifth back to fifth front, maintain the weight over the ball of the supporting foot and keep a space between the toes and the heel.

To execute a battement passé starting from fifth position back, roll through the foot to point sur le cou-de-pied derrière. Slide the inside of the heel up the back of the leg and just before it reaches retiré derrière, lift if over the stick. Touch the little toe in front of the supporting leg, retiré devant, and slide the little toe down to cou-de-pied devant. Separate the foot from the ankle and fold it into fifth position.

Increase the rotation of the working thigh as soon as the foot leaves the floor and maintain pressure on the thigh as the foot moves over the stick. Keep the hips square and the ankle shaped throughout.

Once the working heel lifts to begin either a battement retiré or battement passé, push away from the floor through the first three toes of the working foot even as the weight of the body is held over the ball of the supporting foot. The thigh muscles are perfectly capable of pulling the working foot off the floor, but there are benefits to be gained by allowing the foot to participate in the action. First, the foot is strengthened when it works against the resistance of the floor. Second, the pressure exerted into the floor, if directed through the first three toes, immediately shapes the foot as it leaves the floor. Lastly, the energy gathered from the floor can be used to direct the working foot toward its destination and, later, to assist the supporting leg during a relevé, a pirouette, and a passé sauté.

Work on shaping each section of a battement passé before putting the sections together with music.

> Begin in fifth position with the arm in low fifth. Use a slow duple or triple-meter or work half-time to a quicker tempo. Prepare the arm to second position through middle fifth. Lift the heel (1)/point sur le cou-de-pied devant (2)/move up the leg (3)/over the stick (4)/down the back of the leg (5)/sur le cou-de-pied derrière (6)/move the foot over the footprint (&)/toes/ball (a-7)/heel (8). Reverse and repeat all.

Dégagé en l'air en fondu

From fifth position, prepare the arm to second position and execute a battement tendu à la seconde. Keeping the torso upright, lift the working leg as the standing knee bends and lower the working leg to pointe tendue as the supporting knee straightens.

Control the action of the supporting knee so the fondu reaches the basement at the same time as the working leg reaches the top of the dégagé and so the knee straightens at the same time as the working foot returns to pointe tendue. Focus as much on the depth and alignment of the fondu as on the height of the working leg.

> Begin in fifth position with the arm in low fifth. Use a slow triple-meter. Prepare the arm to second position through middle fifth. Battement tendu quatrième devant (a-1-&)/rond de jambe à terre en dehors (a-2-&)/through first position to tendu quatrième devant (a-3-&)/fifth position (a-4)/battement tendu à la seconde (a-5-&)/dégagé en l'air en fondu (a-6-&)/pointe tendue à la seconde (a-7-&)/fifth position back (a-8). Reverse and repeat all.

Be a detective, constantly on the lookout for a foot that is not properly shaped. When the ankle is not aligned with the leg, besides being aesthetically displeasing, it is dangerous. Severe sprains can occur when landing on a sickled foot from a jump, and tendonitis may develop when the foot bevels or flags, pinching the outside of the ankle.

Execute dégagé en l'air en fondu en croix when the class is ready.

> Begin in fifth position with the arm in low fifth. Use a slow triple-meter. Prepare the arm to second position through middle fifth. Battement tendu quatrième devant (a-1-&)/dégagé en l'air en fondu (a-2-&)/ pointe tendue quatrième devant (a-3-&)/fifth position (a-4)/battement tendu à la seconde (a-5-&)/dégagé en l'air en fondu (a-6-&)/pointe tendue à la seconde (a-7-&)/ fifth position back (a-8). Reverse and repeat all.

Demi-grand rond de jambe en l'air en dehors and en dedans

Demi-grand rond de jambe en l'air can be used in combination with rond de jambe à terre or as part of an adage. Introduce the easiest pathway, first moving the leg side to front, followed by front to side, and then side to back and back to side.

Normally the height of the working leg should increase, not decrease, as it moves from one position to the next. Until the standing side is strong enough to resist the movement of the working leg, however, the working leg should be kept at the same level throughout and raised no higher than 45 degrees.

When moving the leg from front to side or side to front, keep the flowerpot upright and the hips square. When moving from side to back, shift the torso forward so that the working leg is able to move to the back. To achieve the proper line of the leg, knee facing to the side, allow the rotation of the leg to open the working hip. When moving from back to side, rotate the leg, bringing the heel in front of the foot, the body upright, and the hips square.

> Begin in fifth position with the arm in low fifth. Use a slow triple-meter. Prepare the arm to second position through middle fifth. Battement tendu à la seconde (a-1-&)/dégagé en l'air (a-2-&)/demi-rond de jambe en dedans (a-3-&)/fifth position front (a-4)/battement tendu quatrième devant (a-5-&)/dégagé en l'air (a-6-&)/demi-rond de jambe en dehors (a-7-&)/fifth position front (a-8). Repeat.

Reverse the above exercise and then combine the two.

> Begin in fifth position with the arm in low fifth. Use a slow triple-meter. Prepare the arm to second position through middle fifth. Battement tendu quatrième devant (a-1-&)/dégagé en fondu (a-2-&)/pointe tendue quatrième devant (a-3-&)/fifth position (a-4)/battement tendu quatrième devant (a-5-&) dégagé en l'air (a-6-&)/demi-rond de jambe en l'air en dehors (a-7-&)/fifth position back (a-8). Reverse and repeat all.

Attitude en l'air devant and derrière

During the first year, the class learned how to shape an attitude à la seconde from a dégagé en l'air. During the second year, introduce attitude à la seconde, quatrième devant, and quatrième derrière starting with the foot pointed sur le cou-de-pied devant or derrière.

To lift the leg attitude quatrième devant from cou-de-pied devant, move the foot straight front, leading with the heel. To return, open the thigh and, at the same time, draw the little toenail back to the ankle.

To move to an attitude à la seconde from cou-de-pied devant, lift the knee. Because rotation increases as the foot separates from the supporting ankle, note that the bottom half of the leg will move slightly in front of the knee, heel in front of the foot. Return the foot to point cou-de-pied devant or derrière, depending on the movement that follows.

To open to an attitude quatrième derrière from cou-de-pied derrière, lift the knee from under the thigh, like a waiter lifting a tray of dishes, placing the foot in line with the shoulder. Shift the torso forward so that the leg is able to lift in back of the body. Keep the knee even or higher than the foot no matter the height of the thigh. Remember that the hip does not open to rotate the leg; the leg rotates and opens the hip.

Make sure the body does not tilt to the side as the working thigh lifts. Keep the sides even and parallel and the shoulders even and level. Rest the hand on the barre lightly to allow the torso to shift and to give the supporting side the opportunity of resisting the rotation of the working leg.

To return the working foot to the ankle from attitude quatrième derrière, pull the inside of the heel to the back of the calf and bring the body upright. Rotate the top of the leg to resist the action of the bottom half of the leg.

> Begin in fifth position with the arm in low fifth. Use a slow triple-meter. Prepare the arm to second position through middle fifth. Lift heel (&)/point en l'air (a)/sur le cou-de-pied devant (1-&)/attitude quatrième devant (a-2-&)/sur le cou-de-pied devant (a-3)/separate little toe from ankle (&) toes/ball (a)/ heel (4)/dégagé à la seconde (a-5-&)/fondu sur le cou-de-pied devant (a-6-&)/extend à la seconde (a-7-&)/fifth position back (a-8). Reverse and repeat all.

> Begin in fifth position with the arm in low fifth. Use a slow triple-meter. Prepare the arm to second position through middle fifth. Battement tendu quatrième devant (a-1-&)/dégagé en l'air (a-2-&)/attitude quatrième de-vant (a-3-&)/extend quatrième devant (a-4-&)/pointe tendue quatrième devant (a-5-&)/fifth position front (a-6)/demi-plié (7-&)/straighten (a-8). Repeat 2 times en croix.

Continue to sustain the energy of a movement even when the pulses of the meter are implied rather than written.

Rond de jambe en l'air en dehors and en dedans

Rond de jambe en l'air makes use of the battement retiré position and a dégagé en l'air, both introduced during the first year. Pair these two steps in the following exercise before tackling the concept of drawing a "circle" with the bottom half of the leg.

> Begin in fifth position with the arm in low fifth. Use a triple-meter. Prepare the arm to second position through middle fifth. Dégagé en l'air à la seconde (a-1-&)/retiré at the side of the knee (a-2-&)/extend à la seconde (a-3-&)/fifth position front (a-4). Repeat 8 times.

In the above exercise, feel the supporting side activate as soon as the ball of the working foot presses into the floor to begin the dégagé. The supporting side should never be taken by surprise. It should stand ready to resist and balance the working leg as it lifts and rotates. Students should be able to execute the preparatory dégagé as if the barre is not there.

As the working foot opens at the end of a rond de jambe, stretch the underside of the knee and the top of the ankle on the count, but understand that the working leg, like a piece of elastic, continues to pull out of the working hip during the pulses that follow. To balance this powerful stretch, push down through the ball of the supporting foot with equal energy.

Correct

When the class is ready, introduce rond de jambe en l'air. The name of this step can be confusing. Even though the word "rond" is translated as "circle," there is no circle to be found in rond de jambe en l'air. The structure of the knee allows the foot to draw a curve out and to the front when moving to and from an extension to the side, but should it draw a curve out and to the back, the thigh is forced to rotate inward. Therefore, to execute a rond de jambe en dehors (out) starting from a preparatory degage en l'air à la seconde, bring the foot to the side of the knee in a straight line and then draw a curve to the front as the foot returns à la seconde. To execute a rond de jambe en dedans (in), draw a curve to the front to bring the foot to the side of the knee, and then open the foot in a straight line to return à la seconde.

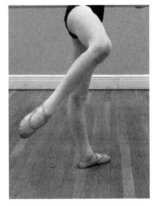

Incorrect

When the foot is positioned at the knee ready to extend à la seconde, open the bottom half of the leg to the height of the knee. As with all extensions that unfold, the knee should never drop to the height of the extending foot. Even when students are advanced enough to lift the knee at the end of a single, double, or at the end of a series of rond de jambe en l'air in order to create a visual or musical accent, still, the bottom half of the leg should open to the height set by the knee.

Begin in fifth position with the arm in low fifth. Use a triple-meter. Prepare the arm to second position through middle fifth. Dégagé en l'air à la seconde (a-1-&)/rond de jambe en dehors (a-2-&)/extend (a-3-&)/fifth position back (a-4)/dégagé en l'air à la seconde (a-5-&)/rond de jambe en dedans (a-6-&)/extend (a-7-&)/fifth position front (a-8). Repeat 8 times.

Once students are able to execute a rond de jambe en l'air correctly, combine the step with dégagé en fondu, grand battement, or battement fondu.

Battement fondu sur le cou-de-pied devant and derrière

In anticipation of a battement fondu sur le cou-de-pied devant, stand in fifth position with the body weight over the ball of the back foot. Raise the front heel and, as the foot peels off the floor through the first three toes to point in front of the ankle, bend the supporting knee. Reach the basement at the same time the little toenail makes contact with the ankle.

To return the working foot to fifth front, separate the foot from the supporting ankle and fold it into the footprint of fifth position. Press the ball of the foot into the floor to straighten both knees.

Both mental and physical effort causes the neck to hold a great deal of tension during both sustained as well as accented movement. The student who works with the weight on the heels, with a weak center, or with the shoulders behind the hips, is forced to grip the muscles of the neck and shoulders just to stay upright. To help identify rigidity in the neck, use the finger test. As you move along the barre or stand near a dancer in the center, push a dancer's head with the tip of your finger. It should give in easily to your touch.

Before executing battement fondu sur le cou-de-pied derrière, remember to separate the toes of the back foot from the supporting heel so that the back knee does not run into the front leg when the working heel lifts. No other adjustments are necessary. As soon as the foot peels off the floor through the first three toes to point en l'air, bend the supporting knee, reaching the basement at the same time as the inside of the heel makes contact with the calf. Make sure to point the foot diagonally toward the floor, in line with the working knee.

To return the working foot to fifth back, move the toes over the footprint and fold the foot into the floor. Press into the floor through the ball of the foot to help both lower the heel and straighten the knees.

When each part of the fondu can be performed clearly and consistently, move from one part to the next without stopping. Use the breath, inhaling as the weight shifts and exhaling as the supporting knee bends.

> Begin in fifth position with the arm in low fifth. Use a triple-meter. Prepare the arm to second position through middle fifth. Battement tendu à la seconde (a-1-&)/dégagé à la seconde (a-2-&)/pointe tendue à la seconde (a-3-&)/fifth position back (a-4)/lift heel (5-&)/point en l'air (a) fondu sur le cou-de-pied derrière (6-&)/move the foot over the footprint (a)/toes/ball (7-&)/heel/knees (a-8). Reverse and repeat all.

Extending attitude en l'air from battement fondu sur le cou-de-pied

As soon as the class is able to execute a fondu sur le cou-de-pied devant and derrière, begin to study how to transition through those positions to and from attitude à la seconde, attitude quatrième devant and attitude quatrième derrière.

To open to an attitude from a fondu, move the working leg away from the ankle before the supporting knee begins to straighten because the foot has farther to go than the knee. To return, bend both knees in unison but control the fondu so that supporting leg reaches the basement at the same time the working foot reaches the ankle.

> Begin in fifth position with the arm in low fifth. Use a triple-meter. Prepare the arm to second position through middle fifth. Use a triple-meter. Lift heel (1-&) point en l'air (a)/fondu sur le cou-de-pied devant (2-&-a)/move working foot away from ankle (3-&-a)/straighten supporting knee as working leg arrives attitude à la seconde (4-&-a)/begin to bend supporting knee as working foot approaches ankle (5-&-a)/fondu sur le cou-de-pied derrière (6-&)/move the foot over the footprint (a)/toes/ball (7-&) heel/knees (a-8). Reverse and repeat all.

Use the above combination to open to attitude devant and derrière from the ankle and, later, to a full extension à la seconde, quatrième devant, and quatrième derrière. To open to a full extension, move the working leg first so that both knees are able to straighten at the same time. To finish, either lower the working leg directly to fifth position or bend both knees at the same time, transitioning through a fondu sur le cou-de-pied before closing fifth. Learning to coordinate the legs in this way prepares for ballonné and battement fondu relevé en effacé.

Use fewer counts as the class advances.

> Begin in fifth position with the arm in low fifth. Use a triple-meter. Prepare the arm to second position through middle fifth. Use a triple-meter. Lift heel (&)/ point en l'air (a)/fondu sur le cou-de-pied devant (1-&)/extend quatrième devant (a-2-&) fondu sur le cou-de-pied devant (a-3)/move the foot over the footprint (&)/toes/ball (a) heel/knees (4). Repeat en croix.

Arabesque

During the second year, many new steps that involve extending the leg to the back are introduced. These include battement dégagé, battement piqué, dégagé en l'air, attitude, and demi-rond de jambe en l'air. As soon as you notice that your students are able to execute these steps with clarity and strength, begin to study how to elevate the working leg above 45 degrees.

Because the students are already accustomed to shifting the body forward when the leg extends behind the body, show them how this shift increases in proportion to the height of the working leg. Demonstrate, also, what happens if the torso fails to make this adjustment, how the working leg gets stuck, how it runs into the wall of its own joint. Point out the V, shaped by the torso and the working leg, one side drawn from under the breast to the top of the supporting leg, the other side drawn by the underside of the lifted thigh. Show how the profile of an arabesque, viewed with the torso on the right and the working leg on the left, looks like a seesaw that tilts to the right when the leg lifts and to the left as the torso comes upright.

To practice the shift, stand in front of a student and provide support by taking her hands as she executes a battement tendu quatrième derrière from first position. Instruct the student to lift the leg and at the moment you feel the leg hit the wall of the hip joint, pull the student forward. Make sure that the forward shift responds to the logjam of the leg and hip socket, not in anticipation of it, and that the logjam is maintained as long as the leg is lifting.

Continue to maintain the logjam as the body comes upright and the leg lowers. When the torso reaches its initial shifting point, release the tension and pointe tendue. Bring the torso to vertical as the working leg returns to first position.

To help a student understand the concept of lifting the working leg from under the thigh, ask her to stand in first position, facing the barre, more than arms distance away, arms extended to the front, shoulder level, so that as she shifts forward in response to the elevation of the leg, she will be able to reach the barre for support. After the student executes a battement tendu quatrième derrière, place your hand under her thigh and lift the working leg like a waiter lifting a tray.

Even though the supporting leg hinges at the hip joint to shift the torso, the angle between the standing leg and the pelvis must not shorten. When this occurs, the V-shape of the arabesque is lost. Pretend that a set of mini-abdominals is at work deep in this angle, lifting the pelvis away from thigh.

To study the upper body, face the mirror. Work individually, allowing the student to rest the leg on a low chair or piano bench so that she doesn't run out of steam while you are fiddling around. Even though many schools ask students to place the working foot in line with the center of the body, I prefer that it

Correct   *Incorrect*

extend behind the same shoulder. An open arabesque puts less stress on the lower back than a crossed position.

Very often, the upper body is pulled into the rotation of the working leg to the extent that the ribs on the standing side poke out. To resist the pull, poke the ribs back in to spiral the upper body. When the spiral of the upper body equals the rotation of the leg, note that the shoulders should be level, squared to the front, and aligned with the sides.

Grand battement en croix

Introduce grand battement quatrième derrière once the class is able to shift and spiral the upper body as the working leg lifts and rotates behind the same shoulder. Perform grand battement en croix when the class is ready. Continue to use four counts for each battement.

Stretching

Along with the floor stretches learned during the first year, introduce gentle, hands-on stretching en l'air, beginning à la seconde and moving on to quatrième devant and quatrième derrière.

Ask the student to place one hand lightly on the barre and extend the leg pointe tendue à la seconde. Take hold of the calf, making sure that your grasp does not interfere with the stretch of the knee or the shape of the ankle. Remind the dancer to stand and remain standing on the blue circle of the supporting foot.

The working leg should rest in your hands, fully rotated but relaxed. As you lift the leg, if you feel the student grip or turn-in, pause and make corrections before proceeding. You want the dancer to not only recognize the full extent of her turn-out but to understand, also, that extension is first about line and then about height. Toss the extended leg up in the air a few inches and then catch it. The leg should feel light and free.

When working with individual students, you will notice that as you fix one thing, something else goes wrong. Like stuffing a suitcase with balloons, push one in and another pops out. When you want the working leg to rotate more, the standing leg turns-in and the working side follows the rotation of the pelvis. Fix the standing leg and the upper body, and, sure enough, the working leg turns in. Perseverance is the only solution.

You will also learn from experience that a correction can be exaggerated to the point that the body is distorted rather than fixed. Something good can actually lead to something bad. This is very true of corrections applied to the arabesque. An instructor might advise a dancer to keep her back up when she observes her leaning too far forward as the leg lifts. This correction aptly describes what needs to be done, but the dancer might react by arching back like a horse when the reins are pulled tight. Very often it is not what you say that really counts but what is actually heard. Certain instructions might produce results for one dancer but not another. Sharpening your visual powers will enable you to see how your words are being interpreted, to recognize when they are ineffective, and, if needed, to find a new way of communicating an idea.

When the leg meets resistance at the top of the stretch, lower the extension somewhat and ask the dancer to hold the shape. If strength is not yet available, reassure the student that it will come eventually. Emphasize that time and the power of mind and imagination will lead to success.

As the students understand the process of stretching, let them stretch each other while you supervise. Stretch one on one even in the intermediate and advanced levels. So much can be observed, corrected, and understood using this method.

Relevés

By the end of the first year of training, the students are able to perform the elevé and relevé in first and second positions both at the barre and in the center as well as a soussus to fifth position demi-pointe at the barre. By the end of the second year, these same students will be executing a single pirouette from fifth position. How do they get from A to Z? The answer lies in introducing various relevés in a logical progression, moving from the easiest to the most difficult, performing these relevés in the center as soon as they are mastered at the barre, and finally, increasing the number of repetitions in order to build strength. This same method will be used when the students begin to work en pointe.

1. **2 feet to 2 feet to 2 feet**

   Included in this category are the elevé, relevé, and soussus. To review, an elevé is executed by lifting the heels to reach demi-pointe and then lowering them, all the while keeping the knees straight.

   A relevé is executed by bending the knees, lifting the heels to straighten the knees, and bending the knees to lower the heels. A relevé can roll up and down or spring up and roll down.

   The soussus is a spring to fifth position demi-pointe beginning and ending in a demi-plié in fifth position. At the top of the relevé, one leg with two heels is visible. Descending, the ball of the front or back foot moves over the footprint of fifth position, the knees bend, and the heels lower.

2. **2 feet to 2 feet to 1 foot**

   A soussus from demi-plié fifth position followed by a fondu sur le cou-de-pied is representative of this category. Begin in fifth position, facing the barre. Execute a demi-plié and soussus to fifth position demi-pointe. From demi-pointe, roll the front foot off the floor to point sur le cou-de-pied devant, shifting the weight of the body onto the back leg. During the shift, make sure to keep the supporting heel as high as it can go, pressing through the ball of the foot into the floor. Counterbalance the downward energy of the supporting leg with a deep abdominal scoop.

   With the working foot pointed at the ankle, bend the supporting knee. At the bottom of the fondu, reach for the footprint with the toes and roll through the foot to fifth position. Push into the floor through the ball of the foot to straighten the knees.

> Begin in fifth position with the right foot front, both hands on the barre. Use a triple-meter. Demi-plié (1-&-a)/soussus (2)/point sur le cou-de-pied devant (a-3)/hold (&-a-4-&-a)/bend the supporting knee (5-&-a)/lower heel (6)/move the foot over the footprint (a)/toes/ball (7-&)/heel/knees (a-8). Repeat 4 times.

Repeat the same combination, starting with the back foot, and then alternate the two. Remember to touch the supporting ankle with the little toenail when the foot is pointed sur le cou-de-pied devant and surround the back of the supporting calf with the inside of the working heel when the foot is pointed sur le cou-de-pied derrière.

3. 1 foot to 2 feet to 2 feet

The simplest version of a relevé that begins on one foot, rises to two feet, and returns to two feet is the battement soutenu relevé. Prepare by extending the working leg à la seconde en fondu, à terre or en l'air. Remember to rotate both legs equally and to maintain the weight of the body over the ball of the supporting foot. Lift the supporting heel and begin to straighten the supporting knee so that the working leg has room to move under the pelvis to shape fifth position demi-pointe, one leg with two heels. From demi-pointe, execute a demi-plié by moving the working leg over the footprint of fifth position, bending the knees, and lowering the heels to the floor at the same time. Straighten the knees by pressing into the floor through the balls of the feet.

> Begin in fifth position with the right foot front, both hands on the barre. Use a triple-meter. Dégagé à la seconde en fondu with the right foot (a-1-&-a)/soutenu to fifth position demi-pointe, right foot front (2-&)/move the foot over the footprint (a)/demi-plié fifth position (3-&)/straighten (a-4). Repeat with the back leg, closing fifth position back. Repeat all.

A more complex relevé found in this category begins with a battement fondu sur le cou-de-pied devant or derrière, moves to fifth position demi-pointe, and finishes in a demi-plié fifth position.

> Begin in fifth position with the right foot front, both hands on the barre. Use a triple-meter. Lift back heel (1-&)/point en l'air (a)/fondu sur le cou-de-pied derrière (2-&)/lift supporting heel (a) fifth position demi-pointe (3-&-a, 4-&-a)/move the back leg over the footprint (5-&-a)/demi-plié fifth position (6-&)/straighten (a-7)/hold (&-a-8). Repeat 4 times.

As students progress, use fewer counts.

> Begin in fifth position with the right foot front, both hands on the barre. Use a triple-meter. Lift back heel (&)/pointe en l'air (a)/fondu sur le cou-de-pied derrière (1-&-a)/fifth position demi-pointe (2-&)/move the back leg over the footprint (a)/demi-plié fifth position (3-&)/straighten (a-4). Repeat 4 times.

Change meters.

> Begin in fifth position with the right foot front, both hands on the barre. Use a duple-meter. Lift back heel (&)/pointe en l'air (a)/fondu sur le cou-de-pied derrière (1)/fifth position demi-pointe (&-2)/move the back leg over the footprint (&)/demi-plié fifth position (3)/straighten (4). Repeat 4 times.

Note that all relevés in this category prepare for the pas de bouree.

4. 2 feet to 1 foot to 2 feet

Use the exercise below to introduce a relevé onto one leg.

> Begin in fifth position with the right foot front, both hands on the barre. Use a strong duple-meter. Demi-plié in fifth position (1)/relevé sur le cou-de-pied devant (2)/reach for footprint with working foot (&)/demi-pliè fifth position (3)/straighten (&-4). Repeat 4 times.

During the preparation, place the weight on the ball of the back foot to make sure that the relevé will be as close to vertical as possible. Without shifting the weight onto the front foot, push through the balls of both feet and spring up onto the back foot, reaching demi-pointe and touching the little toenail in front of the ankle at the same time. Open the working thigh against the resistance of the supporting side.

To come down, reach for the footprint of fifth position with the toes of the front foot. Release the toes into the floor, bend the knees, and lower both heels at the same time.

Introduce a relevé sur le cou-de-pied derrière in the same way.

Before introducing relevé retiré devant, practice moving the working foot to that position starting from fifth position demi-pointe. Slide the little toenail up the shin until it reaches as high as the flexibility of the knee and working hip allow. Maintain the height and shape of the supporting ankle and the supporting heel as the working foot changes position and as the working thigh opens.

From retiré devant, slide the working foot down the front of the supporting leg, release the toes of the working foot into the footprint of fifth position, bend the knees, and lower the heels.

To execute a relevé retiré devant, again, begin with the weight over the ball of the supporting foot in the starting fifth before the demi-plié. Assist the spring with the ball of the working foot, take both heels off the floor at the same time, and travel vertically. Rotate the working thigh and resist rotation with the supporing side. Reach the knee with the little toenail of the working foot at the same time the supporting foot reaches the penthouse.

To return to demi-plié fifth position, lower the working foot, release the toes into the footprint of fifth position, bend the knees, and lower both heels to the floor at the same time.

> Begin in fifth position with the right foot front, both hands on the barre. Use a strong duple-meter. Demi-plié (1)/relevé retiré devant (2)/demi-plié fifth position front (&-3)/straighten (&-4). Repeat 4 times.

Like the relevé retiré devant, stand on demi-pointe and practice the path of the working foot before introducing a relevé retiré derrière and a relevé passé.

> Begin in fifth position with the right foot front, both hands on the barre. Use a strong duple-meter. Demi-plié (1)/relevé passé (2)/demi-plié fifth position back (&-3)/straighten (&-4)/battement tendu à la seconde (&-5)/grand battement (6)/pointe tendue à la seconde (&-7)/fifth position front (&-8). Repeat 4 times.

5. 1 foot to 2 feet to 1 foot

Anticipate the repetition of each of the exercises below by maintaining the weight of the body over the ball of the supporting foot even as the working foot closes in fifth position and the knees straighten.

> Begin in fifth position with the right foot front, both hands on the barre. Use a triple-meter. Dégagé à la seconde en fondu with the right leg (a-1-&-a)/soutenu fifth position demi-pointe, right leg front (2-&)/point sur le cou-de-pied devant (a-3-&,a-4-&-a)/fondu (5-&-a)/move the foot over the footprint (6-&-a) toes/ball (7-&)/heel/knees (a-8). Repeat 4 times.

> Begin in fifth position with the right foot front, both hands on the barre. Use a triple-meter. Lift back heel (1-&)/point en l'air (a)/fondu sur le cou-de-pied derrière (2-&)/lift supporting heel (a)/fifth position demi-pointe (3-&-a,4-&-a)/point sur le cou-de-pied derrière (5-&-a)/fondu (6-&)/move the foot over the footprint (a)/toes/ball (7-&)/heel/knees (a-8). Repeat 4 times.

6. 1 foot to 1 foot to 2 feet

Among the relevés found in this category, two are appropriate for beginning students. The first is a battement fondu relevé sur le cou-de-pied, devant or derrière, finishing in fifth position.

> Begin in fifth position with the right foot front, both hands on the barre. Use a duple-meter. Battement fondu sur le cou-de-pied devant (&-1)/relevé (2)/demi-plié fifth position (&-3)/straighten (&-4). Repeat 4 times.

From the bottom of the fondu, lift the supporting heel and, pushing into the floor through the ball of the foot, straighten the supporting knee to raise the body upward. At the top of the relevé, reach for the footprint of fifth position with the working foot and then bend both knees at the same time, finishing in fifth position demi-plié. Straighten the knees, placing the weight on the ball of the back foot, ready to repeat the exercise.

The second type appropriate for beginners is a relevé à la seconde.

> Begin in fifth position with the right foot front, both hands on the barre. Use a duple-meter. Battement fondu sur le cou-de-pied devant (&-1)/relevé à la seconde (2)/demi-plié fifth position, right foot front (&-3)/straighten (&-4). Repeat 4 times.

As the supporting heel releases to begin the relevé, move the working foot away from the ankle. Straighten both knees at the same time as the supporting foot reaches the penthouse and the working leg reaches à la seconde. Lower the working leg, bringing the ball of the foot over the footprint of fifth position, and then bend the knees and lower both heels to the floor at the same time. As the knees straighten, place the weight over the ball of the back foot ready to repeat the exercise.

Introduce the combinations found in this category and the next at the end of the second year or during the third year, depending on the skill of the students.

7. 1 foot to 1 foot to 1 foot

Perform this type of relevé in a series. Start from fifth position with the weight over the ball of the front or back foot and execute a battement fondu sur le cou-de-pied derrière. From the bottom of the fondu, lift the heel of the standing leg, pushing into the floor through the ball of the foot and begin to straighten the knee to raise the body upward. At the top of the relevé, bend the supporting knee and lower the heel, continuing to maintain the weight over the ball of the foot in anticipation of the relevé that follows. Repeat the same action with each relevé and fondu, heel/knee going up, knee/heel going down, weight on top of the ball of the supporting foot to insure a consistent, vertical rise.

> Begin in fifth position with the right foot front, both hands on the barre. Use a crisp duple-meter. Battement fondu sur le cou-de-pied derrière (&-1)/relevé (2)/fondu (&-3)/relevé (4)/fondu (&-5)/relevé (6)/demi-plié fifth position (&-7)/straighten (8). Wait eight counts and begin again.

Remember to make a dynamic contrast between the two movements of a relevé. Accent the rise and control the descent.

Cambré side, front, and back

Even though a cambré to the side, front, and back, are usually introduced during the second year, some classes may be ready for a cambré side, using the arm, by the end of the first year. The object of a cambré is to warm up and increase the flexibility of the spine.

Initiate a cambré side by leading the arm from the wrist out of low fifth or second position. Draw a broad arc and, as the arm nears the head, begin to bend up and over the top of the ribcage, (the rim of the flowerpot). At the finish of the cambré, turn the working hand over to shape high fifth, framing the head as if the body was erect. Reach through the curve of the arm to stretch the working side. At the same time, keep the neck and head in line with the spine, hold the shoulder down, and increase the pressure through the balls of the feet to counterbalance the stretch.

Until the students understand how to hinge from the hip correctly, practice the cambré front with the hand at the waist. Begin the movement with a deep breath, lifting the chin and the focus slightly. Bend forward with the back flat but, as soon as the stretch becomes too intense, round the body and then the head over an imaginary barrel. Use the weight of the head to pull the body down and in toward the legs.

Continue to maintain the weight of the body over the balls of the feet at the bottom of the stretch. Do not rock back on the heels. An elevé should be possible, even in this awkward position.

Reverse the order of the forward bend to return to an upright position. As the spine elongates, move the head in line with the spine, increase pressure through the balls of the feet, and hinge at the hips to bring the body on top of the legs.

When a port de bras is added to the forward bend, use the initiating breath, not only to open the chest and lift the head but to activate the arm as well. After turning the hand and lengthening the fingers, sweep the arm through a long curve at the same time the body begins to hinge at the hips. At the moment the body rounds over the imaginary barrel and the forehead moves close to the legs, fold the hand in to complete the shape of high fifth, upside down.

To return to vertical, hinge at the hips, elongate the spine and increase pressure through the balls of the feet. By the time the torso is parallel to the floor, the back of the neck should be in line with the spine and the arm should be in high fifth. From parallel, the table position, bring the torso, arm, and head upright as a unit. Help set the torso on top of the legs by stretching the upper arm out of the back. Even as the arm pulls away from the body, keep the upper arm rotated and the shoulder down.

Moving up through a flat back puts a great deal of strain on the lower back. Some teachers prefer beginning students to roll up through the spine to a standing position. In that case, move the arm through middle fifth, reaching high fifth as the body returns to vertical.

Once upright, inhale to initiate a cambré to the back. Elongate the spine, scoop the abdominal muscles, and with the arm placed slightly in front of the head, shoulder down and upper arm rotated, pull the arm out of the back, again increasing the pressure exerted through the balls of the feet in order to maintain balance.

Correct   *Incorrect*

It is important to understand that the object of a cambré back is to increase the flexibility of the upper spine, the source of artistic expression. To this end, think of the legs drawing a vertical line that starts at the top of the ribs and extends through the floor. From this base, begin the curve midway between the shoulder blades and let it flow out the top of the head. Make sure the head does not fall into the shoulders as it moves behind the body. From the side, the cambré should take the shape of a candy cane or an upside down J. Note that when the spine curves below the shoulders, the weight of the body moves into the pelvis and the thighs as a way of balancing the weight of the upper body hanging behind it. As a result, the lower back is severely compressed.

When the body returns to vertical, open the arm directly to the side from in front of the head. Once the students advance, they will learn to move the arm to second position by stretching the arm out of and behind the same shoulder.

Battement tendu, using the arm and the head

Up to this point, the class has learned where to focus at the beginning and end of an exercise, how to turn and incline the head, how to use the head during the preparation of the arm, and how to circle the head from position A to position C through position B. Use this knowledge in the following exercises.

Begin in fifth position, arm in low fifth, head turned and inclined away from the barre (position A), eyes focused in the direction of the nose. Use a triple-meter. Battement tendu quatrième devant, arm to middle fifth, head turned and inclined to the barre (position C), eyes focused into the palm (a-1-&)/fifth position, arm to low fifth, head turned and inclined away from the barre (position A), eyes focused in the direction of the nose (a-2-&-a)/demi-plié (3-&)/straighten (a-4). Repeat 2 times en croix.

Begin in fifth position, arm in low fifth, head turned and inclined away from the barre (position A), eyes focused in the direction of the nose. Use a triple-meter. Demi-plié, arm to middle fifth, head turned and inclined to the barre (position C), eyes focused into the palm (1-&)/battement tendu quatrième devant, arm to second position, head turned and inclined away from the barre (position A), eyes focused in the direction of the nose (a-2)/extend the arm through second position (3-&)/fifth position, arm to low fifth, chin over the mid-line (position B), eyes focused into palm (a-4-&-a), ready to continue. Repeat 2 times en croix.

When the head reaches position C, turned and inclined to the barre, keep the chin lifted even though the eyes are focused into the palm. At the end of the exercise, do not follow the hand as it returns to low fifth. Instead, keep the head turned and inclined away from the barre (position A) and continue to focus in the direction of the nose.

Begin in fifth position with the arm in low fifth, head turned and inclined away from the barre (position A), eyes focused in the direction of the nose. Use a triple-meter. Prepare the arm to second position through middle fifth. Battement tendu quatrième devant (a-1-&)/arm to high fifth (position D), eyes focused into palm (a-2-&)/fifth position (a-3)/open arm to second position, head turned and inclined away from the barre (position A), eyes focused in the direction of the nose (a-4). Repeat 2 times en croix.

When the arm reaches high fifth in the above exercise, look into the palm of the hand, not only with the eyes, but with the whole face, as if looking into a mirror. Label this position D, an addition to the ABC series.

When the arm returns to second position from high fifth, turn and incline the head away from the barre (position A), eyes focused in the direction of the nose.

When the arm finishes in second position at the end of an exercise, move it through second to low fifth but keep the head turned and inclined (position A), eyes focused over the nose.

Begin in fifth position with the arm in low fifth, head turned and inclined away from the barre (position A), eyes focused in the direction of the nose. Use a triple-meter. Prepare the arm to second position through middle fifth. Move through second position on the first pulse (&), following the last count of the preparation, and bend the elbow on the second pulse (a). Move the arm to low fifth, chin over the mid-line (position B), eyes focused into palm (1)/battement tendu quatrième devant, arm to high fifth (position D), eyes focused into palm (a-2-&-a)/demi-plié fifth position, arm to middle fifth, head turned and inclined to the barre (position C), eyes focused in into the palm (3-&)/straighten, arm second position, head turned and inclined away from the barre (position A), eyes focused in the direction of the nose (a-4)/move through second position (&)/bend the elbow (a), ready to continue. Repeat 2 times en croix.

As the arm moves from high to middle fifth, keep the shoulders level and make sure the fingertips remain on the outside of the center line.

Begin in fifth position with the arm in low fifth, head turned and inclined away from the barre (position A), eyes focused in the direction of the nose. Use a triple-meter. Prepare the arm to second position through middle fifth. Battement tendu quatrième devant (a-1-&)/arm to high fifth (position D), eyes focused into palm (a-2-&-a)/demi-plié fifth position, arm to middle fifth, head turned and inclined to the barre (position C), eyes focused into palm (3-&)/straighten, arm to second position, head turned and inclined away from barre (position A), eyes focused in the direction of the nose (a-4). Repeat 2 times en croix.

Begin in fifth position with the arm in low fifth, head turned and inclined away from the barre (position A), eyes focused over the nose. Use a triple-meter. Prepare the arm to second position through middle fifth. Move through second position on the second pulse (a) following the last count of the preparation. Demi-plié, arm low fifth, chin over mid-line (position B), eyes focused into palm (1-&)/battement tendu quatrième devant, arm to high fifth (position D), eyes focused into palm (a-2-&)/arm to second position, head turned and inclined away from the barre (position A), eyes focused in the direction of the nose (a-3)/fifth position (a-4)/move arm through second position (a), ready to continue. Repeat 2 times en croix.

In the above exercise, bend the elbow and knees at the same time on the count of one.

Begin in fifth position with the arm in low fifth, head turned and inclined away from the barre (position A), eyes focused over the nose. Use a triple-meter. Move the foot out of fifth position and the arm through middle fifth, head turned and inclined to the barre (position C), eyes focused into palm (a)/battement tendu quatrième devant, arm to high fifth (position D), eyes focused into palm (1-&)/fifth position, arm to low fifth, chin over mid-line (position B), eyes focused into palm (a-2)/demi-plié, arm demi-seconde, head turned and inclined away from the barre (position A), eyes focused over the hand (3-&)/straighten, arm to low fifth, chin over mid-line (position B), eyes focused into palm (a-4), ready to continue. Repeat 2 times en croix.

In the above exercise, find the hand as it reaches middle fifth and follow it, like a butterfly, throughout the exercise. As the hand unfolds in demi-seconde, lift the chin slightly being careful that this action does not limit the depth of the demi-plié.

Begin in fifth position with the arm in low fifth, head turned and inclined (position A), eyes focused in the direction of the nose. Use a triple-meter. Battement tendu quatrième devant en fondu, arm to middle fifth, head turned and inclined to the barre (position C), eyes focused into palm (a-1-&)/straighten, arm to second position, head turned and inclined away from the barre (position A), eyes focused in the direction of the nose (a-2-&)/fifth position (a-3)/move arm through second position to low fifth, chin over mid-line (position B), eyes focused into palm (a-4-&), ready to continue. Repeat 2 times en croix.

Correct   *Incorrect*

In the above exercise, keep the back straight during the battement tendu quatrième devant en fondu and do not let the fingers of the working hand cross center as the head inclines toward the barre.

Battement tendu, alternating legs

Alternating legs during a combination gives students the opportunity of adjusting to weight changes early in the class, before moving to the center.

Begin in fifth position with the arm in low fifth. Use a duple-meter. Prepare the arm to second position through middle fifth. Battement tendu à la seconde (&-1)/fifth position back (&-2)/battement tendu à la seconde (&-3)/fifth position front (&-4)/battement tendu à la seconde (&-5)/fifth position back (&-6)/battement tendu quatrième devant, inside leg (&-7)/fifth position (&-8). Reverse and repeat all.

Begin in fifth position with the arm in low fifth. Use a duple-meter. Prepare the arm to second position through middle fifth. Battement tendu quatrième devant (&-1)/fifth position (&-2)/battement tendu à la seconde (&-3)/fifth position back (&-4)/battement tendu quatrième derrière (&-5)/fifth position (&-6)/battement tendu quatrième devant, inside leg (&-7)/fifth position (&-8). Reverse and repeat all.

Begin in fifth position with the arm in low fifth. Use a duple meter. Prepare the arm to second position through middle fifth. Battement tendu quatrième devant (&-1)/fifth position (&-2)/repeat (&-3)/(&-4)/quatrième derrière with the inside leg (&-5)/ fifth position (&-6) battement tendu à la seconde, outside leg (&-7) fifth position back (&-8). Reverse and repeat all.

Remember, with each shift, the weight goes immediately to the ball of what will be the supporting foot.

Piqué en avant to fifth position demi-pointe

Once the class has mastered the soussus, knows how to shape fifth position en demi-pointe and how to descend from that position to a demi-plié, introduce piqué en avant to fifth position demi-pointe. Practice at the barre in the beginning. The word "piqué" means to prick or pick, but the action of a piqué is best described by the word "perch," meaning to land on, like a bird on a branch.

> Begin in fifth position with the arm in low fifth. Use a slow triple-meter. Prepare the arm to second position through middle fifth. Dégagé en l'air quatrième devant en fondu (a-1-&)/piqué quatrième en avant to fifth position demi-pointe (a-2)/move front leg over footprint (a)/demi-plié fifth position (3-&)/straighten (a-4). Repeat 4 times.

Standing in fifth position before the preparatory dégagé in the above combination, anticipate the piqué by placing the weight of the body over the ball of the back foot. Following the first count, move through the fondu and push off the ball of the supporting foot on the pulse (&). Leave the floor for a brief moment before landing on the front leg on the following pulse (a) and closing fifth position with the back leg on the count (2).

Be able to balance a book on top of the head from the beginning of the piqué to the end. Placing the extended leg on the floor and dragging the back foot to fifth position is the most common mistake made by beginning students. As a result of this action, the body tilts forward before the piqué and arches back after the piqué.

Make sure that both legs rotate equally during the fondu preparation and as the weight is transferred. Land on the front leg with the inside of the heel forward and pull the back leg into fifth position demi-pointe from the inside of the thigh.

Use the barre for light support only at the beginning and end of the piqué. During the piqué, move the arm with the shoulder, sliding the hand over the top of the barre.

When the students are ready to practice the exercise, form a line at one end of the barre. When one student completes four piqués, let the next one begin.

Piqué en avant to retiré derrière

Executing a piqué en avant to retiré derrière prepares for the piqué turn en dehors. Introduce the step once the class is able to perform a piqué to fifth position without the barre, correctly shape retiré derrière, and stand securely at the barre on one leg on demi-pointe. With the exception of the final position, transfer the body from one leg to the other in the same way it is transferred from one leg to two.

As the ball of the supporting foot pushes away from the floor, direct the inside of the heel to the back of the knee. Touch the heel to the knee at the same time the body alights on demi-pointe. Open the thigh while keeping the hips square.

Again, practice the step moving from one end of the barre to the other. Let each student execute four piqués before the next one begins.

Begin in fifth position with the arm in low fifth. Use a slow triple-meter. Prepare the arm to second position through middle fifth. Dégagé en l'air quatrième devant en fondu (1-&-a)/piqué retiré derrière, quatrième en avant (2)/demi-plié fifth position (3-&)/straighten (a-4). Repeat 4 times.

In order to land on the second count in the above combination, move through the bottom of the fondu preparation and push off of the ball of the supporting foot on the second pulse (a), following the first count.

2   IN THE CENTER

During the second year, bring each new step mastered at the barre to the center and begin to combine them in interesting and challenging ways with what is already known.

Positions of the body

The nine positions of the body include croisé, quatrième and effacé devant, ecarté devant, à la seconde, and ecarté derrière, and effacé, quatrième, and croisé derrière. Each position is determined by the way the body faces (straight front or diagonally front), the direction of the working leg (front, side, or back), and which leg is used (right or left). As you demonstrate the positions, define the new terms, croisé, ecarté, and effacé and explain how to differentiate between croisé and effacé by looking into the mirror to see if the legs are crossed (croisé) or open (effacé). Start with croisé devant and move clockwise.

When working diagonally, avoid facing the front corner of what is usually a rectangular classroom. Facing that corner turns the dancer away from the audience, seated behind and beyond the mirror. It is like facing the downstage wing of a stage. Instead, think of facing the corner of an imaginary square, surrounding the body. This image helps to sharpen the diagonal and turn the dancer more toward the audience.

Working within a square also makes it possible for a group of dancers to execute the same position and look alike despite the shape of the space. For example, if you ask a line of dancers to execute battement tendu croisé devant facing the corner of the room, each one will need to turn a little more or a little less, depending on their position in the line. As a result, they will all look different even though they are executing the same position. If you ask everyone to face the corner of their own square, however, the line of dancers will look identical.

Even as you concentrate on one position, continue to review the others until the students are able to recognize and name each one. There is no timetable. Only make sure that the students can shape a position clearly and consistently standing in place before using it in combination with other steps, before adding a new position, or before learning how to execute a step, such as sissonne tombée, en diagonal.

1. **Fifth position croisé**

   Draw a square on the floor with chalk or tape. Stand in the middle of the square in fifth position, feet placed at equal angles, arms in low fifth, and with the head inclined to the right shoulder. Look in the mirror for signposts that indicate if the body is facing correctly. Be able to see the heel of the front foot, a space between the body and the rounded left arm, and a diamond at the bottom of a demi-plié. If the body faces correctly in the starting position, the movement that comes from that position will also face correctly.

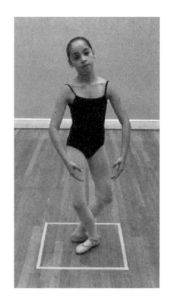

2. **Battement tendu croisé devant**

   Stand in the imaginary square in fifth position croisé devant with the right foot in front and fold the arms in front of the body. From there, execute a battement tendu croisé quatrième devant. The inside of the heel, calf, and thigh of the extended leg should be visible in the mirror.

   Once the students understand the placement of the lower body, add the arm position most commonly used by beginners, high third. Study the position, one arm at a time.

   Place the arm opposite the extended leg overhead and draw a C-curve to frame the head. Rotate the upper arm and hold the shoulder down to reveal a U-shape between the neck and the arm.

   To taper the curve of the arm, rotate the wrist so that only the side of the little finger is seen by the audience. To prevent the hand from drooping, open the wrist and reach up toward the center line with the tips of the fingers.

   Extend the other arm to the side of the body and draw the perfect curve of second position. If the arm appears foreshortened because of the angle of the body, stretch the arm back from the shoulder until the palm of the hand can be seen in the mirror.

   It is expected that beginners will execute the battement tendu croisé devant academically. As a dancer advances, though, the position should come alive. From a simple breath, the torso should spiral slightly toward the audience, the upper back should arch, lifting the face, and the side arm should stretch back from the shoulder to open the chest. Demonstrate the full beauty of the finished position so the class understands what lies ahead.

3. *Battement tendu effacé devant*

To prepare for battement tendu effacé devant, face the right corner of the square. Place the back foot on a diagonal, making sure the inside of the heel is visible, and then place the front foot on an equal angle to shape fifth position.

Once the correct viewing angle is set and the shoulders and hips are aligned on top of the legs, extend the working leg out from the right shoulder. Make sure both legs rotate equally.

Again, position the arms in high third, placing the arm opposite the working leg overhead. Rotate the upper arm to frame the face and rotate the wrist to hide the palm. Open the wrist and elongate the fingers to lengthen the curve and, at the same time, hold the shoulder down so that the U-shape between the neck and the arm can be seen.

As you teach the positions of the body, note that the facing of croisé devant and ecarté devant are determined by the angle of the working heel while the facing of croisé derrière, effacé devant and derrière, and ecarté derrière are determined by the angle of the supporting heel.

If the curve between shoulder and neck or the inside of the supporting heel cannot be seen in the mirror as a dancer poses pointe tendue croisé derrière, arms in high third, do not ask her to distort some part of her body to correct the shape. Instead, move her body, like a figure standing on a turntable, more toward the front.

Realize that the aesthetic line is more than a physical attribute. It is an illusion achieved by manipulating how the body is viewed from the audience.

Ecarté devant

Ecarté derrière

Crosé derrière

Effacé derrière

Arm positions for first, second, and third arabesque à terre

During the second year, continue to refine the arm positions that define first, second, and third arabesques. When the dancers are strong enough, shape the arms with the leg extended en l'air.

1. First arabesque

Extend the arm on the supporting side to the front and the other arm to the side to form a right angle. Without locking the elbows, draw straight lines with the arms. Allow the wrists to drop ever so slightly.

Once the right angle is established and the lines of the arms are drawn correctly, move the side arm slightly to the back until a stretch is felt in the front of the shoulder. Make sure the movement of the arm does not effect the position of the shoulders or the spiral of the upper body.

2. Second arabesque

Practice second arabesque at the barre. Light support allows the dancer to better feel the connection between the arm extended to the front and the leg extended to the back. Place the outside leg in fifth position back and the working arm in middle fifth so that both limbs have the same distance to travel and can arrive in position at the same time. As the working leg moves out of fifth, turn the hand over and lead the arm into a straight line, extending diagonally from the shoulder. Make sure the elbow does not lock.

Reach through the arm to help the body shift as the working leg extends to the back. The stretch of the arm should balance the stretch of the working leg, but without affecting the working shoulder or the elbow. Use a rubber band to illustrate how the two forces are opposite yet equal.

Correct

Incorrect

Position the chin parallel to the line of the extended arm and focus the eyes in the direction of that line. Note that if the hand is placed too high and the focus follows, the dancer will be tempted to lean back.

From second arabesque, recover by returning the arm to middle fifth and bringing the body upright with the head erect at the same time the working leg closes fifth position back.

3. Third arabesque

Third arabesque is the arm position commonly used with a grand jeté. Both arms are held, equidistant, in front of the body, one parallel to the floor and the other reaching upward on a diagonal.

Practice shaping the position facing the mirror. Stand in fourth position and let the arms hang loosely from the shoulders at the sides of the body, palms to the rear. From there, lift the arms into position, and like a window, look through them. Lift the chin slightly and focus the eyes to the horizon.

TRANSITION STEPS  3

The transition steps taught during the second year begin to give beginners a sense of dance. Finally they are starting to move more, up and down and side to side. Memory, concentration, and endurance are all challenged by the length of the combinations. Class livens up a bit.

Glissade changée

Glissade changée is a transition step that travels to the side and changes feet. Monitor the start and finish of the step in fifth position, making sure that both legs rotate equally in the V-shape. When moving to the side, right or left, changing feet or not, determine the direction of the glissade by the diagonal placement of the working foot.

Begin in fifth position with the right foot back, arms in low fifth. Use a duple-meter. Demi-plié on the last count of the preparation. Glissade changée (&-1)/changement (&-2)/échappé sauté (&-3,&-4). Repeat to the other side. Repeat all.

Begin in fifth position with the right foot back, arms in low fifth. Use a duple-meter. Demi-plié on the last count of the preparation. Glissade changée (&-1)/relevé passé, arms to middle fifth (2)/demi-plié fifth back, arms to low fifth (3)/changement (&-4). Repeat to the other side. Repeat all.

Glissade en avant

Glissade en avant is a connecting step that travels to the front in the direction of the front foot.

Hold the weight of the body over the ball of the back foot both in the starting fifth and during the preparatory demi-plié. As the front leg begins to brush out of fifth position, push off the floor from the back foot, moving the body forward through a low arc. At the top of the arc, straighten both knees at the same time to form a wide V. Land a little beyond the front foot and immediately slice the back leg into fifth position demi-plié.

Maintain a strong center to prevent the torso from reacting to the forward thrust of the back leg.

Begin in fifth position with the right foot front, arms in low fifth. Use a duple-meter. Prepare the arms to second position through middle fifth. Demi-plie (1)/glissade en avant (&-2)/straighten (3)/ hold (4). Repeat 4 times.

Pas de bourrée dessous from pointe tendue à la seconde

A pas de bourrée is a transition step that is used to cover space, change direction, turn the body around, and/or change the position of the feet. Once the class learns how to rise on one leg to fifth position demi-pointe, introduce pas de bourrée dessous. Initiate the step first from a dégagé à la seconde en fondu and then from a fondu sur le cou-de-pied derrière.

In the beginning, practice the pas de bourrée dessous at the barre. Students need light support to help balance while they learn to articulate the parts of the step.

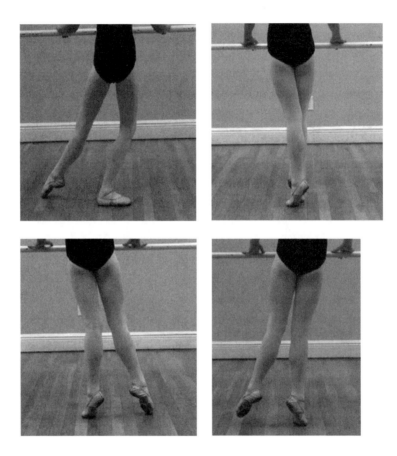

> Begin in fifth position with the left foot back, both hands on the barre. Use a slow triple-meter. Battement tendu à la seconde en fondu with the left leg (a-1-&)/begin to lift the supporting heel (a) rise to fifth position demi-pointe, left foot back (2-&)/extend right leg (a) step right, extending the left leg (3-&-a)/ demi-plié fifth position, left foot front (4-&), straighten (a-5)/hold and prepare to repeat other side (6-8). Repeat all.

A pas de bourrée is a walking step. It may start and finish on two legs, but in between, the body balances fully, first on one leg and then on the other leg. To successfully transfer the weight of the body, make sure the side-step does not move beyond the shoulder of the same leg. As one leg supports the body, extend the other leg just enough to stretch the foot and rotate the leg à la seconde.

As the knees straighten from the demi-plié, shift the weight to the ball of the front foot to prepare for a pas de bourrée dessous starting with the other leg. Work slowly and without music to make sure that each step is on balance and each position is shaped correctly.

Use the words "dessous" and "dessus" to describe the action of the working leg, the leg extended side in the preparation, in relationship to the supporting leg. It doesn't matter if the working leg begins in front or in back in the starting fifth position. If it extends side and closes in back when the legs come together in fifth position demi-pointe, then the pas de bourrée is described as dessous. The working leg finishes under or behind the supporting leg. If, however, the working leg moves over or on top of the supporting leg, the pas de bourrée is described as dessus.

The subtleties of the pronunciation of "dessous" and "dessus" are very difficult to master. If your lips can't manage to distinguish between the sounds, "ous" and "us", use the English translation, "over" and "under." Just make sure your students know the differences between the two French terms.

When the combination given at the top of this section is brought to the center, make sure the tempo of the music is slow enough to allow a clear execution of the pas de bourrée but not so slow as to make it impossible to balance. Work half-time to a quick triple-meter. The quantity of notes will buoy the dancer.

Place the arms in second position to support balance. Later, when the class is ready, add a port de bras to the same combination. Start with the arms in low fifth and prepare to second position through middle fifth. Turn the palms over on the first step through fifth position demi-pointe. Move the arms through second position on the second step. Bend the elbows to lower the arms to low fifth at the same time the knees bend to lower the body to fifth position demi-plié. Lift the arms through middle fifth as the knees straighten, open the arms to second position, and hold before repeating the combination to the other side.

Once the pas de bourrée can be performed correctly, combine with other steps.

Begin in fifth position with the right foot back, arms in low fifth. Use a duple-meter. Battement tendu à la seconde en fondu with the right leg (&-1)/begin to lift the supporting heel (&) pas de bourrée dessous (2,3)/demi-plié fifth position, right foot front (4)/glissade derrière (&-5)/changement two times (&-6)/(&-7)/straighten (8). Repeat to the other side. Repeat all.

Begin in fifth position with the right foot back, arms in low fifth. Use a quick triple-meter. Prepare the arms to second position through middle fifth. Dégagé en fondu with the right leg (a-1-&) begin to lift the supporting heel (a)/pas de bourrèe dessous (2-&-a,3-&-a)/demi-plié fifth position, right foot front, rounding right arm to form middle third (4-&-a)/relevé

retiré devant (5-&-a)/demi-plié fifth position, right foot front (6-&)/glissade devant (a-7)/straighten, opening the rounded arm to second (8). Repeat to the other side. Repeat all.

Pas de bourrée dessous from fondu cou-de-pied derrière

When you introduce pas de bourrée dessous from fondu sur le cou-de-pied, first review how to move the foot from fifth position back to point at the ankle and how to rise from one leg to fifth position demi-pointe. Practice at the barre before working in the center.

Begin in fifth position with the right foot back, both hands on the barre. Use a triple-meter. Lift the back heel (1-&)/point en l'air (a) fondu sur le cou-de-pied derrière (2-&)/begin to lift the supporting heel (a)/step onto the right foot through fifth position demi-pointe (3-&-a)/step left (4-&-a)/demi-plié fifth position, right foot front (5-&)/straighten (a-6)/shift weight and prepare to repeat other side (7-&-a,8-&-a). Repeat all.

Repeat the above exercise using fewer counts.

Begin in fifth position with the right foot back, both hands on the barre. Use a duple-meter. Lift the back heel (&)/point en l'air (a) fondu sur le cou-de-pied derrière (1)/begin to lift the supporting heel (&)/step onto the right foot through fifth position demi-pointe (2)/step left (3)/demi-plié fifth position (4)/straighten (5)/prepare to repeat other side (6-8). Repeat all.

Move the above combination to the center and add a simple port de bras. Prepare the arms to second position. Round the right arm to third position during the fondu, open the right arm to second as the supporting leg raises the body to fifth position demi-pointe, and hold both arms in second until the exercise repeats to the other side.

Next, increase the difficulty level of the port de bras.

Begin in fifth position with the right foot in back, arms in low fifth. Use a duple-meter. Lift the heel of the back foot, carrying the arms to middle fifth (&)/ point en l'air (a)/fondu sur le cou-de-pied derrière, opening the left arm to second position (1)/begin to lift the supporting heel (&)/step right onto the right foot through fifth position demi-pointe and begin to open the right arm to second position (2)/step left, moving both arms through second position (3)/bend the knees to return to demi-plié fifth position, right foot front, and bend the elbows to lower the arms to low fifth (4)/straighten (5)/hold and prepare to repeat other side (6-8). Repeat all.

TURNS 4

Pirouette en dehors from fifth position

At the end of the first year, students learn how to execute a battement retiré devant and derrière and a battement passé standing flat. When a relevé is added to each of these steps during the second year, first at the barre and then in center, the connection between these steps and the pirouette emerges. Begin to study the mechanics of turning only when all relevant skills have been learned and practiced repeatedly, when each student knows how to use the floor to go up and come down, has the strength to stand on one leg en demi-pointe and sustain balance, and understands how to rotate both legs with equal energy.

A pirouette en dehors may be introduced at the barre or in the center, but in my experience students seem to find their balance faster when they don't have anything to grab onto for support. I also choose not to break a pirouette en dehors into quarter and half turns. I find that a dancer tenses the body as a way to stop short at the end of a quarter or half turn when she should actually be learning how to use the body to complete and later sustain the end of a full turn.

> Begin in fifth position with the right foot front, arms in low fifth. Use a slow triple-meter. Lift the arms to middle fifth on the last count of the preparation. Hold (1-&)/demi-plié, opening the left arm to the side (a)/ relevé retiré devant, arms middle fifth (2-&-a)/demi-plié fifth position, right foot front (3-&)/ straighten (a-4)/repeat three times (5-8,1-4)/hold (5-&)/ demi-plié, opening the left arm to the side (a)/relevé passé, arms middle fifth (6-&-a), demi-plié fifth position, right foot back (7-&)/straighten (a-8). Repeat to the other side.

To better connect the demi-plié to the relevé, assign it only one pulse (a). When the class is ready, replace the relevé passé with a pirouette en dehors.

Introducing the pirouette from fifth position is beneficial for two reasons. First, it is easier to get on top of the supporting leg because it is already close to the center line. There is more risk preparing from fourth or second position because the dancer must move the body to the supporting leg or move the supporting leg under the body. Second, by restricting the feet in fifth, the dancer learns to rely more on the feet, the arms, and the working leg as power sources. More strength is required, and, therefore more strength is developed.

There are as many ways of teaching a pirouette as there are teachers. Normally we teach what worked for us as dancers. The key is to stay open to new information, to learn from your own analysis and experimentation, and to be secure enough to make changes in your approach. Offer a basic, consistent method to beginners, but as students progress in their training, give them as much information to work with as possible. In this way students are able to discover over time what works for them.

The following information applies specifically to a pirouette en dehors that begins and ends in fifth position.

1. *Preparation*

As with any step, the success of the pirouette is determined, in part, by the correctness of the preparation. In the standing fifth, place the weight on the ball of the back foot, relevé-ready. During the demi-plié, keep the weight over the ball of the back foot as the thighs open. Remember that a demi-plié is effective only if it is deep and controlled and connects seamlessly to the relevé that follows.

2. *Relevé*

The goal of the relevé is to set the body on top of the supporting leg so that a turn or turns may be accomplished in a specific division of time. The amount of power available to the legs and feet, whose task it is to lift the body, comes from the preceding demi-plié. The phrase, "go down to go up," describes the essential connection between the two actions.

Without shifting the weight of the body off the ball of the supporting foot during the demi-plié, push away from the floor with the ball of the working foot.

Make sure that the supporting heel does not swivel to the back at the start of the relevé. Maintain rotation by lifting both heels off the floor at the same time. Leave the floor just enough to allow the ball of the foot to move even closer to the center line and alight on the highest demi-pointe possible, the penthouse.

3. *Balance*

A series of actions and reactions are needed to sustain balance on top of the supporting leg long enough to complete a full turn. Respond to the energy

exerted into the floor through the ball of the supporting foot by rotating the upper arms and contracting the abdominal muscles. Resist the working thigh, moving toward the back, and the working foot, moving up the leg, by rotating the upper arm on the supporting side. Stabilize the pelvis by contracting the abdominal muscles and rotating the legs. Allow the upper arms to rotate by keeping the shoulders down.

4. Rotation and resistance

You may hear a teacher instruct a pupil to lead with the knee or get the knee behind the shoulder during the pirouette. These suggestions are meant to encourage maximum rotation of the working thigh, one of the main turning forces of the pirouette. This force is effective, however, only to the extent that the supporting side, from heel to shoulder, resists it. The side that pushes the body around must have something to push off of.

5. Arms

It has already been mentioned how the arms work to balance the body. In a pirouette, they are also used to help turn the body. Begin a pirouette en dehors to the right with the arms in middle third, the right arm rounded and the left in second position. Moving from the preparation, close the left arm to middle fifth as the feet push away from the floor and as the supporting thigh opens. If the left side lags behind, it will become an anchor, holding the body back.

6. Head

Once on balance, it is the quick whipping movement of the head that determines the number of turns and the musicality of each one. This quick movement is called spotting, first discussed in relation to chaînés turns, introduced the first year. To spot, hold the focus on one specific point as the turn begins and then whip the head around to find that same spot before the turn is actually completed.

Spotting can be practiced by performing the following exercise. Face front, look into the mirror, and focus eye level. Using the heels as a pivot point, begin turning to the right, taking small steps. Maintain the head and focus to the front until the head can no longer hold its position, about midway through the turn, and then whip the head around to face and focus in the mirror once again. Make sure that the head does not tilt as it whips around.

7. Finish

Ideally, the end of a pirouette is sustained before the dancer returns to earth. All the elements required to balance work a little harder. Abdominals scoop more deeply, the upper arms rotate a little more, the supporting leg pushes deeper, the supporting side puts on the brakes to resist the momentum of the turn, and the foot at the knee lifts higher before moving over the stick to return to fifth back. The phrase, "go up before you go down," describes the moment before the end of a pirouette. For beginning students, however, returning the working foot to its starting position underneath the pelvis, fifth back, at the end of the turn, touching the floor with both heels at the same time and on a specific note of the music are more realistic goals.

In contrast to the strong accent of the relevé, the side arm, and the head, the finish of the pirouette is soft and controlled, providing an interesting visual dynamic. As the knees bend coming out of the pirouette, catch hold of the floor with the ball of the working foot, placing it behind the supporting heel. Lengthen the spine and maintain a strong center to lighten the body. As the heels lower, support the weight of the body on the balls of one or both feet, depending on the step that follows.

8. Synthesis and coordination

A pirouette comes together on top of the leg as a result of different forces unleashed from the preparation. Each technical detail of the pirouette is important, but success will depend on how well all these details come together.

9. Musicality

The voice that calls all the parts together emanates from the brain, responding to the rhythms and accents of the music. Every part of a pirouette has a relationship with the music and moves fluidly through or accents a particular note.

Begin in fifth position with the right foot front, arms in low fifth. Use a slow triple-meter. Lift the arms to middle fifth on the last count of the preparation. Hold (1-&)/demi-plié fifth position, opening the left arm to the side (a)/pirouette, middle fifth (2-&-a)/demi-plié fifth position, right foot back (3-&)/straighten (a-4. Repeat to the other side. Repeat all.

As your students practice pirouettes, make corrections, but at the same time, encourage them to think analytically, to identify and solve a problem using the information they have learned. The body is sometimes able to bypass the brain and self-correct, but conscious thought produces results that are long-lasting.

Chaînés turns

During the first year, chaînés turns are practiced at the end of the class, just for fun. The students hold their hands on their shoulders, elbows extended straight to the side, and spin down an imaginary diagonal line extending from one corner to the next. During the second year, continue performing chaînés turns with arms on the shoulders, but apply what has been learned during the second year to this series of chaînés turns.

Walk into fifth position in the upstage back corner, place the arms on the shoulders, and extend the front leg tendu croisé devant. From the preparation, execute a low dégagé en fondu on the pulse before the first count. On the first count of the phrase, spring off the supporting leg and at the same time move the working leg over the diagonal line to accept the weight of the body. Work on maintaining a high demi-pointe, narrow the space between steps, and keep a steady tempo, one count per step. Place a decal or object eye level in each corner so that the students can use it for spotting.

5 PETITE ALLEGRO

Sissonne simple

The first challenge of the sissonne simple is to draw the legs together in a well-shaped fifth position at the top of the jump. The second challenge is to land, balanced on one foot, to ensure a smooth and efficient transition into the next step.

> Begin in fifth position with the right foot back, arms in low fifth. Lift the arms to middle fifth on the third count of a four-count preparation. On the fourth count, demi-plié and open the side arm to shape middle third. Use a strong duple-meter. Glissade derrière, landing on the right foot (a)/demi-plié fifth position, left foot front (1)/sissonne simple (&)/land on the left foot, right foot pointed sur le cou-de-pied derrière (2). Continue across the floor.

Make sure that the weight of the body is placed securely on the ball of the left foot at the end of the sissonne simple in preparation for the glissade that follows. To form a V in the air, extend the right foot at the same time the left foot pushes the body through the arc of the glissade.

Remember, pointing in back of the ankle means to surround the lower calf of the supporting leg with the inside of the working heel.

> Begin in fifth position with the right foot back, arms in low fifth. Use a duple-meter. Demi-plié (1)/sissonne simple (&)/land on the left foot, right foot pointed sur le cou-de-pied derrière (2)/pas de bourrée dessous (3-&)/demi-plié fifth position, right foot front (4)/straighten (&). Repeat to the other side. Repeat all.

In the combination above, the link between the sissonne and the relevé that follows is similar to the one between the sissonne simple and the glissade derrière discussed above. The weight of the body is held over the ball of the left foot at the end of the sissonne in preparation for the pas de bourrée dessous that follows. Notice how quickly the supporting heel must come off the floor at the end of the sissonne in order to begin the pas de bourrée on the assigned note.

Pas de chat

Pas de chat, meaning "step of the cat", is yet another step that lends itself to imitation. Hold your hands under your chin like paws and invite the students to follow you as you spring into the air and then return to earth ever so lightly. After the essence of the step is captured, break the step down into its component parts to refine the positions of the legs and feet.

Hold the weight on the ball of the front foot during the starting fifth and the demi-pliè. From the bottom of the demi-plié, peel the back foot off the floor and slide the heel up the back of the leg through retiré derrière. Lift the working knee to the side at the same time the supporting foot springs off the floor. Descend on the right foot and pass the left foot through retiré devant to fifth position front. Remember that the distribution of weight at the end of the pas de chat is determined by the step that follows.

Begin in fifth position with the right foot back, arms in low fifth. Use a duple-meter. On the third count of a four-count preparation, move the arms through middle fifth and on the fourth count, open the left arm to the side to shape third position. Demi-plié (1)/right knee lifts (&)/left knee lifts as right foot lands (a)/ left foot closes front, demi-plié fifth position (2)/ straighten (3)/hold (4). Repeat 3 times, using the last four counts of the second eight to change sides.

Ideally, a diamond is shaped by the legs at the top of the pas de chat. Beginning students, however, do not have enough strength in the lower body nor are they able to coordinate the limbs to lift the hips high enough to achieve this goal. Until they do, expect them to keep the feet under the pelvis and move through a well defined retiré derrière and devant.

Begin in fifth position with the right foot back, arms in low fifth. Use a duple-meter. On the third count of a four-count preparation, lift the arms to middle fifth. On the fourth count, demi-plié and open the left arm to the side to shape third position. Glissade derrière (&-1)/pas de chat (&-2). Continue across the floor.

All the time and attention spent on teaching your class how to shape and move the arms clearly and beautifully will most certainly pay off as the complexity of the allegro portion of the class increases. Note that it is difficult to sculpt once the clay is on the move.

In the previous combination, travel diagonally to the side. Use the back foot to direct the path of the glissade and the working knee to determine the path of the pas de chat. The sharpness of the diagonal will depend on the turn-out of the dancer.

Turn and incline the head to the rounded arm of third position and focus the eyes over the forearm, as if peering over the edge of a cliff—eager to see what lies below, but at the same time, careful not to fall off. Avoid looking into the empty space defined by the arm. The chin drops when the focus is

Correct

Incorrect

drawn into this hole. The audience is unable to see the face and the weight of the head works with gravity against the upward thrust of the jump.

> Begin in fifth position with the right foot back, arms in low fifth. Use a duple-meter. Demi-plié on the last count of the preparation. Glissade derrière, arms to middle third, right arm rounded (&-1)/pas de chat, finishing with the right foot pointed sur le cou-de-pied derrière (&-2)/pas de bourrée dessous, changing arms (&-a)/demi-plié fifth, rounding left arm to middle third (3)/straighten (&)/demi-plié (4). Repeat to the other side. Repeat all.

During the glissade in the preceding exercise, positional changes of both the arms and the legs occur. In order to move efficiently and achieve visual co-ordination, bring the arms to middle third from low fifth, one arm rounded and the other directly to second position, at the same time as the body moves up into space.

Échappé sauté, using the arms

> Begin in fifth position with the right foot front, arms in low fifth. Use a duple-meter. Demi-plié (1)/echappé, arms middle fifth (&)/second position, arms second position (2)/sauté, extend arms through second position (&)/demi-plié fifth position, right foot back, arms to low fifth (3)/straighten (4). Repeat left foot front. Repeat all.

Keep the elbows below the shoulders and the hands below the elbows in both middle fifth and second positions. As the arms move through second position, extend the hands at the same time as the legs shape second position en l'air.

Jeté dessus

Begin jeté dessus with the weight supported over the ball of the front foot. Bend the knees and begin to squeeze the back foot out of fifth position. As the ball of the working foot brushes off the floor, simulating a frappe, push away from the floor with the ball of the supporting foot. The simultaneous explosion of both feet should lift the body high enough so that the legs can draw the V-shape of second position en l'air.

All the energy in a jeté is directed vertically. The step does not travel. To that end, make sure that the working leg never works against the supporting leg. It should not come down as the supporting leg tries to lift the body up nor should it pull more than the supporting leg pushes.

To descend from the top of the jump, bring the working leg under the center line of the torso. Land en fondu as the other knee bends to bring the foot to point sur le cou-de-pied derrière.

When a combination uses both the arms and the legs, demonstrate the combination in its complete form, first, and then break it down to work on the various parts and counts assigned to those parts. Once the foot-work is mastered, review the pathway of the arms several times. Put the arms and legs together by marking the entire combination slowly. Increase the tempo, and finally, add the music.

Remember that marking means to perform the entire combination without actually jumping or turning. Use the upper body, the back, the arms, and the head, with artistry while indicating the shape and direction of the feet and legs.

Begin in fifth position with the left foot front, arms in low fifth. Demi-plié on the last count of the preparation. Glissade derrière (&-1)/jeté dessus (&-2)/pas de bourrée dessous (&-3-&)/demi-plié fifth position, left foot front (4). Continue across the floor.

To initiate the pas de bourrée in the above combination, lift the heel of the supporting foot on the pulse (&) before the third count. Step onto the left foot on the third count and onto the right foot on the pulse (&), following the count.

This combination does not alternate sides but moves across the floor, with the arms held in second position, third, or low fifth. As coordination increases, add the following port de bra. Begin with the arms in low fifth and hold this position during the glissade. Move to third position on the upward movement of the jeté and maintain third position on the landing. During the pas de bourrée, move both arms through second position and, as the knees bend to lower the body to fifth position demi-plié, bend the elbows to lower the arms to low fifth.

When the landing of a jeté becomes secure, alternate glissade jeté to the right and left.

Begin in fifth position with the left foot front, arms in low fifth. Glissade derrière to the right (&-1)/jeté dessus, arms middle third, right arm rounded (&-2)/glissade derrière to the left, arms low fifth (&-3)/jeté dessus, arms middle fifth, left arm rounded (&-4). Repeat all 4 times.

Balance securely on top of the ball of the supporting foot at the end of the glissade to insure easy transition between the end of the jeté and the beginning of the next glissade. Contrast the controlled landing with the explosive jump and make sure there is a difference in height between the V-shape of the glissade and the V-shape of the jeté.

Rotate the upper arms to move them from low to middle fifth. When the upper arms inwardly rotate, the back stretches and widens, lifting the upper body out of the pelvis and off the legs. Lifting the top off the bottom will not only help lighten the jump, but the landing as well.

Increase the number of steps in a combination once the class is comfortable with the mechanics of each individual step. Tempo may also be increased.

Begin in fifth position with the right foot back, arms in low fifth. Demi-plié on the last count of the preparation. Glissade derrière (&-1)/jeté dessus (&-2)/pas de bourrée dessous (&-a)/demi-plié fifth position (3)/changement (&-4). Repeat to the other side. Repeat all.

This combination calls for four different steps within a four-count measure. To help students move with the required speed, emphasize the rhythm of the movement. For example, the above combination can be vocalized as da-da, da, da-da-da, da, each sound signifying the rhythm created when one or both feet touch the floor. Like tap dancing, the rhythm of the music is echoed by the feet connecting to the floor.

Port de bras used in the previous combination may also be added.

> Begin in fifth position with the right foot back, arms in low fifth. Demi-plié on the last count of the preparation. Glissade derrière (&-1)/jeté dessus, moving the arms to middle third, right arm rounded in front (&-2)/pas de bourrée dessous, moving the right arm to second and then extending both through second (&-a) demi-plié fifth position, bending the elbows to bring the arms to low fifth (3)/changement (&-4). Repeat to the other side. Repeat all.

The above combination may be lengthened by adding glissade derrière left (&-5)/assemblé dessus (&-6)/repeat right (&-7)/(&-8). Build on what your students already know. Keep old material alive by bringing it forward and adding the new.

Part III

Elementary 3: Syllabus for the Third Year

During the third year, students most often commit to two classes a week, ninety minutes each. They are older, more focused, more in charge of their bodies. They look forward to going on point. This is the year of rapid, sometimes dramatic progress.

When appropriate, add a balance at the end of an exercise, standing on demi-pointe on one or both legs, or standing flat with the leg extended or pointed at the ankle or knee or on demi-pointe on one or both legs. Challenge the class to maintain clarity even as you increase the tempo or the number of steps in a combination. You will no longer be teaching anything new concerning shape, placement, or balance. You will only be reinforcing what has already been taught and explaining how it supports new material.

Barre exercises:

Battement tendu en croix, using the arm and head

Inclining the head and looking to the side

Battement dégagé, using the arm and the head

Rond de jambe à terre en dedans and en dehors in one count

Preparation of the arm with rond de jambe à terre

Double frappé quatrième devant and derrière

Battement fondu à la seconde, using the arm

Relevés on one foot (see page 104)

Rond de jambe en l'air

Développé à la seconde

Développé à la seconde, using the arm

Développé quatrième devant

Développé quatrième derrière

Grand battement in two counts

Stretching with the leg on the barre

Petite battement sur le cou-de-pied

Soutenu en tournant en dedans (half-turn)

Piqué arabesque

Center exercises:

Detourné d'adage en dehors and en dedans

Detourné d'adage en l'air

Promenade

Pas de bourrée dessus

Temps lié à la seconde, quatrieme en avant, and quatrième en arrière

Chassé en diagonal

Chassé qautrième en avant

Sissonne tombée

Balancé de côté

Soutenu en tournant en dehors

Chaînés turns, using the arms

Piqué turn en dedans

Pirouette en dedans from fourth position

Pirouette en dehors from fourth position

Changement épaulement

Assemblé dessous

Sissonne fermée effacé en avant

Sissonne ouverte effacé en avant

Assemblé devant and derrière

Coupé

Royale

AT THE BARRE

Beginning and ending an exercise

During the first year, the position assumed before an exercise is academic rather than expressive. The dancer stands in first or fifth position with the arm in low fifth and the eyes straight ahead. During the second year, this position is embel-

lished by turning and inclining the head away from the barre and focusing the eyes in the direction of the nose. During the third year, a touch of epaulement is added to give the position more style and elegance. Epaulement is a term used to describe the response of the shoulders to a subtle spiral of the upper back. The head still turns and inclines on top of the neck, but it does so by growing out of and in opposition to the spiral.

Whichever way an exercise ends, return to the starting position. For example, if the arm finishes in second position, bend the elbow to lower the arm and, just as the hand folds in to complete the curve of low fifth, spiral the upper spine toward the barre and turn and incline the head away from the barre, focusing the eyes over the nose. If the exercise finishes with a balance, return to demi-plié fifth position and straighten the knees to set into motion the spiral that turns and inclines the head and changes the focus of the eyes.

The beginning of an exercise gives a dancer time to center the body and bring attention inward. The end of an exercise gives a dancer time to recover and reflect. One is the first impression and the other is the last. Dancers have a tendency to grow careless with how they start and finish their work. Keep your standards high.

Battement tendu en croix, using the arm and the head

Students will be able to coordinate the arm and the head during battement tendu en croix simply by following the hand wherever it goes not only with the eyes but with the nose as well. If the eyes move, the head does not necessarily have to move, but when the nose moves, the head must move. Study the pathways of the arm and head before coordinating them with the series of tendus.

Give special attention to the transition between the preparation and the first tendu quatrième devant. Begin in fifth position, arm in low fifth, head in position A, eyes focused over the nose, and hold four counts of an eight–count preparation. Lift the arm to middle fifth and shift the head to position C to find the palm of the hand (5). As the arm opens to second position, increase the turn and incline of position A to look into the palm of the hand (6). Smell the rose, lifting the face and extending the hand through the ends of the fingers as the arm moves through second position (7). Bend the elbow and circle the head

(5)   (6)

(7)   (&)

down and around (&) to find the palm in low fifth, position B (8). Finally, follow the hand through middle fifth (&) to finish in high fifth, position D, as the leg extends to the front (a–1).

When each section of the transition can be executed correctly, use fewer counts. Hold the first five counts of an eight-count preparation (1–5), lift the arm to middle fifth (6), through second position (7), bend the elbow to return the arm to low fifth (&–8)/ lift it through middle fifth (&) and to high fifth as the leg extends to the front (a–1).

Because the arm has fewer counts to move through second to high fifth, give into gravity as soon as the elbow bends. Drop and swing the arm through low fifth to high fifth. Use the image of heavy gold rings not only to help increase the speed of the drop but to help maintain the length of the curve as well. Follow the hand, moving through position B and C, no matter how fast it travels from one position to another.

From high fifth, position D, lower the arm to middle fifth, position C, eyes focused into palm, as the leg returns to fifth position (&–2).

Extend the leg à la seconde, following the hand from middle fifth through second position (&–3) and again, smell the rose, lifting the face and extending the hand through the ends of the fingers. Bend the elbow to lead the arm to low fifth as the leg returns to fifth position (&–4). Circle the head down through position B, looking into the palm of the hand as it completes the long curve of low fifth.

Before extending the leg quatrième derrière, move the arm to middle fifth on the pulse (&), following the last count (4), so that the arm and leg are able to arrive in second arabesque at the same time on the next count (5).

Remember to draw a straight line with the front arm without locking the elbow or flagging the hand. Use the stretch of the arm to help shift the body forward and to balance the stretch of the leg. Place the fingertips of the extended arm slightly above the shoulder to allow the focus of the eyes and the line of the chin to run parallel with the arm. Later, incline the top of the head slightly away from the barre to soften the position.

(8)   (&)   (1)

From second arabesque, return the leg to fifth back (&-6) and round the arm to middle fifth, eyes to palm, head inclined to the barre in position C. Follow with a second battement tendu à la seconde, this time closing in front (7-8).

When the students are ready, perform battement tendu en croix, using the arm and head, with music. Continue to work slowly until the class is able to coordinate all three parts of the body without losing the shape of any one part.

Other than shape, there are no rules that dictate how an arm or the head should be used during a particular combination. The head and arm are considered ornaments and, as such, can be positioned or moved to a position in a variety of ways. While the port de bras presented above moves through the gateways of middle and low fifth, another instructor might choose to move the arm from one position to another outside of the body, omitting the gateways. Whatever choice you make, however, stick with it during the first three years until your students gain enough control of their bodies to handle change.

(4)   (&)   (5)

Inclining the head, looking to the side

To prepare the students to work and move diagonally in the center, teach them how to focus to the side of the body, turning and inclining the head in opposition to the inside leg as it extends to the front and to the back.

> Begin in fifth position with the arm in low fifth. Use a slow duple-meter. Prepare the arm to second position. Battement tendu à la seconde (&-1)/fifth position back (&-2)/repeat, closing front (&-3,&-4)/repeat, closing back (&-5,&-6)/battement tendu quatrième devant with the inside leg (&-7)/fifth position (&-8). Reverse and repeat all.

During the three battement tendus à la seconde, keep the head erect and the focus front.

When the inside leg extends to the front, keep the torso vertical except for a gentle curve of the upper spine. Like a cambré back, begin the curve from a point midway between the shoulder blades and extend it through the neck to turn and tilt the head. Observe this positioning at the top of a cabriole effacé devant and at the end of a pirouette en dehors that opens développé effacé devant en fondu. It is not only beautiful; it also helps to balance the body when the working leg extends en l'air to the front.

When the body shifts forward over the supporting leg to allow the inside leg to extend to the back, tilt the head forward on top of the neck and turn it to the side away from the barre.

Use the image of peeking in front or behind a tree placed to the side of the working shoulder to help the class understand how to shape both positions. Peek in back of the tree when extending quatrième devant and peek in front of the tree when extending quatrième derrière.

Practice the backward tilt of the head, sitting on the floor cross-legged, facing sideways to the mirror, to develop an awareness of how the tilt affects the balance.

Battement dégagé, using the arm and the head

Once the students are able to execute the battement dégagé closing on the count, perform a series à la seconde, adding a simple port de bras and a coordinated movement of the head.

Begin in first position with the arm in low fifth, head erect, eyes focused front. Use a slow duple-meter. Battement dégagé à la seconde (&)/first position (1). Complete four sets of eight.

On the first four counts of the first eight, lead the arm from the wrist diagonally side and unfold it into a straight line extending above the shoulder. On the second count of four, hold the position of the arm. On the first four counts of the second eight, bend the elbow to return the arm to low fifth and hold that position for the last four counts.

At the end of the first dégagé, as the working foot returns to first position on the first count, find the hand in low fifth. Follow the hand for the next three counts as it rises above the shoulder to the side of the body. Look over the hand for the last four counts of the first eight. On the first four counts of the second eight, follow the hand as it returns to low fifth. On the last four counts of the second eight, bring the head erect and focus front.

This is called a "pat your head and rub your tummy" exercise because the leg and the arm differ in quality and direction. First, practice the pathway of the head and the arm, add the movement of the leg, and then perform with music. Make sure the accent of the foot, as it closes in first position, does not affect the smooth, even carriage of the arm.

Développé à la seconde

Teachers differ somewhat on how to begin a développé. Some want the foot to wrap around the ankle as it comes from fifth position while others prefer the foot to peel off the floor and point directly at the ankle. While both are correct, I prefer that beginning students use only the pointed position until they have more control over their bodies.

Even though a développé is a fluid and continuous unfolding of the leg through several positions, for the sake of clarity, work on each position separately. Begin with the weight already over the ball of the supporting foot, ready to release the working heel from fifth position. Once the working heel lifts, push away from the floor, directing the little toenail to the ankle. Make sure rotation in the hip socket increases as the foot moves from the floor to the ankle and as it moves up the supporting leg to the knee. Keep asking the question, "Is your knee as far side as possible?" Remember that even when the foot pauses at the knee, it does not sit on the knee.

From retiré devant, lift the working knee, pulling the foot away from the standing leg to shape an attitude à la seconde. The height of the working knee in this transitional position determines the final height of the développé. From the attitude, open the bottom half of the working leg à la seconde, as if opening the leg of a card table.

The placement of the foot at the knee depends on where the développé is coming from and where it is going to. If the foot begins in fifth position front and opens à la seconde or quatrième devant, then it will move through retiré devant. The little toenail will touch the knee. If the foot begins in fifth position back and opens à la seconde or quatrième derrière, then it will move through retire derrière. The inside of the heel will touch behind the knee in the shape of a piqué turn. Encourage proper foot shape in all these positions.

Once the leg begins in one direction and moves to another without closing in fifth position, the foot will begin or end retiré devant, little toenail to knee, when extending to or returning from quatrième devant, and the heel will touch in back of the knee to shape retiré derrière extending to or returning from quatrième derrière. The foot touches the side of the supporting knee only when the foot comes in from and then returns to the side during a rond de jambe en l'air or when the foot passes from quatrième devant to quatrième derrière or from quatrième derrière to quatrième devant.

> Begin in fifth position with the arm in low fifth. Use a triple-meter. Prepare the arm to second position. Lift the heel (&)/point en l'air (a) point sur le cou-de-pied devant (1)/slide the working leg retiré devant (a-2)/lift the working leg attitude à la seconde (a-3)/open à la seconde (a-4)/pointe tendue à la seconde (a-5)/fifth position back (a-6)/demi-plié (7-&)/straighten (a-8). Repeat, starting from fifth position back.

In the previous combination, the foot reaches the ankle, the attitude, and à la seconde on the count. The pulse before each of those counts indicates the transition from one position to the next.

Développé à la seconde, using the arm

Once the développé à la seconde has been mastered, add a simple port de bra to the above exercise. Lift the arm from low fifth to middle fifth as the leg moves from the ankle to retiré devant. Open the arm to second position as the leg moves to attitude à la seconde. After the working leg closes fifth position back, omit the demi-plié and instead, extend the arm through second position (7-&), bend the elbow on the next pulse (a) and lower the arm to low fifth (8).

Développé quatrième devant

To maintain the rotation of the leg as it moves from retiré devant to the transional attitude, lead with the inside of the working heel as if serving tea. From the attitude, extend the bottom half of the leg to the height of the knee so that the foot draws a straight line from the shoulder. Make sure that the torso and supporting leg resist the elongation of the working leg.

Développé quatrième derrière

The rotating action that shapes the preparatory retiré derrière also lifts the thigh to the transitional attitude and maintains the line of the leg as it extends behind the shoulder. If the working foot leads the leg to attitude, the knee will drop and rotation will be lost.

Shift the torso to counterbalance the attitude and then increase the shift slightly when the bottom half of the leg opens to the height of the knee. To maintain balance as the knee stretches, exert equal pressure into the floor through the supporting leg. In addition, deepen the abdominal contraction to hold the ribs together and prevent the back from arching.

Remember that there is a limit to how far the torso moves forward. Draw a V with the torso and the thigh of the working leg in both the attitude and the

arabesque that follows. Maintain a continuous tension between the two sides of the V. The working leg should say to the torso, "I want to go up. You go down!" The torso should say, "No, I want to stay up. You go down!"

Note that a similar struggle occurs between the supporting side and the working leg. The rotation of the working leg, like a powerful magnet, pulls the supporting side toward it. The standing leg turns in, the working side shortens, and the ribs on the supporting side stick out. Fight this force by engaging the oblique abdominals on the supporting side to retract the ribs and spiral the upper body. To achieve balance, the spiral of the upper body should equal the rotation of the working leg.

Grand Battement in two counts

By the third year, execute a grand battement using two counts, one to go up and one to come down. Because the leg is now moving into the air directly from fifth, not from a shaped tendu, stress the importance of increasing rotation as the working foot slides away from the supporting foot. If the leg rotates before it lifts, all the muscles used to rotate the leg become available to lift it. If the leg is not rotated, the number of muscles that can be relied upon to lift decreases and, as a result, the leg feels heavy and constricted as it goes up.

No matter the direction of the battement, remember to go up fast and come down with control. Be careful not to grip the barre and, consequently, the neck. Maintain a contraction of the abdominal muscles to absorb the energy of the kick.

Make sure that the pressure exerted into the floor through the supporting leg equals the energy of the kick. Use that same pressure to elongate the supporting leg and, thus, lift the body away from the floor so that the working leg has room to return to fifth position with the knee straight.

Once grand battement can be performed in two counts en croix, combine with other steps.

> Begin in fifth position with the arm in low fifth. Use a strong duple-meter. Prepare the arm to second position. Grand battement quatrième devant (1)/ fifth position (&-2)/repeat (3,&-4)/demi-plié (5)/relevé passé (6)/demi-plié fifth position back (7)/straighten (8)/grand battement à la seconde (1)/fifth position front (&-2)/grand battement à la seconde (3)/fifth position back (&-4)/demi-plié (5)/soussus (6)/demi-plié (7)/straighten (8). Reverse and repeat all.

Double frappé quatrième devant and derrière

When introducing a battement double frappé, quatrième devant and derrière, review the isolation exercise practiced during the second year. Place the leg in a 45-degree attitude à la seconde. Relax the bottom half of the leg, including the foot, and move the leg in and out several times, hinging at the knee. Repeat with the foot flexed to show how hinging becomes a double beat.

Remember, the working leg is able to move in and out quickly, without affecting the neck and arm, only if the contraction of the abdominal muscles and the rotation of the legs work together to stabilize the pelvis. Demonstrate how a double frappé relates to a royale or an entrechat quatre.

Extend the foot from a double beat the same way the foot extends from a single. To the front, place the ball of the foot on the floor and brush, leading with the heel. To the back, open the thigh, pulling the foot away from the ankle to bring the side of the big toe in contact with the floor, and brush, leading with the knee. Maintain the shape of the foot during each beat, the brush, and the extension. Avoid the Achilles tendon by beating only the inside and the outside of the supporting ankle with the inside and outside of the working foot.

> Begin in fifth position with the arm in low fifth. Use a slow duple-meter. Prepare the arm to middle fifth on the third count of a four-count preparation. Open the arm to second position and execute a battement tendu à la seconde on the fourth count. Battement single frappe en croix (1-4)/double frappe en croix (5-8). Reverse and repeat all.

Use a pulse and a count to indicate the beat and the brush of a single frappe (&-1). Use two pulses and a count to indicate the two beats and the brush of a double frappé (&-a-1).

At the end of the exercise, balance with the leg à la seconde, standing flat, or soutenu to fifth position and balance on demi-pointe. At the end of the balance, demi-plié in fifth position and bring both arms to low fifth. As the knees straighten, spiral the upper back and turn and incline the head away from the barre, eyes focused over the nose.

Petite battement sur le cou-de-pied

Normally the foot is held in the wrapped position during this step, but again, because the position distorts the shape of the ankle, I prefer that beginning students execute the step with the foot pointed until the intermediate level.

The action of the working leg during petite battement sur le cou-de-pied is similar to a double frappé. The thigh maintains rotation as the bottom half of the leg moves in and out, hinging at the knee.

Begin with a preparation pointe tendue à la seconde. On the pulse preceding the count, execute a low dégagé en l'air and, allowing the leg to give in to gravity, beat the front of the ankle on the count. Use the rebound to move the leg to a low attitude, in position for the second beat in back of the ankle.

Maintain the shape of the pointed foot, beating in front of the ankle with the little toenail and then in back of the lower calf with the inside of the heel.

As with all beats, use the big muscle groups, the rotators and abdominal muscles, to stabilize the pelvis and absorb the energy of the beats.

> Begin in fifth position with the arm in low fifth. Use a staccato duple-meter. Execute a battement tendu à la seconde on the last count of the preparation. Dégagé en l'air (&)/petite battement sur le cou-de-pied front and back (1-6)/beat front (7)/pointe tendue à la seconde (8)/dégagé en l'air (&)/petite battement sur le cou-de-pied back and front (1-6)/beat back (7)/pointe tendue à la seconde (8). Repeat all 4 times.

At the end of the exercise, take both arms to middle fifth, dégagé en l'air à la seconde, and balance. At the end of the balance, demi-plié in fifth position and return to the starting position as the knees straighten.

Rond de jambe à terre in one count

By the third year, combine rond de jambe à terre with one or more of the following: battement dégagé, passing through first position, attitudes in different directions extending from the ankle, battement dégagé en fondu, battement retiré, and battement soutenu en relevé. Because rond de jambe à terre is performed early in the barre, keep the tempo slow and extensions at 45 degrees.

When rond de jambe à terre en dehors is given two or four counts, the working foot has enough time to reach a full point, quatrième devant, before the leg circles to the back. When the step is given only one count, however, the foot must necessarily push away from the center line on that count before reaching a full point. The rotating leg needs the energy of the foot to help it move quickly around to the back and through first position to begin the next rond de jambe on the following count.

Push away

As the working leg moves en dehors past second position, lift out of the supporting hip by increasing the contraction of the abdominal muscles and exerting more pressure into the floor through the supporting foot. This action, along with a forward shift, makes room for the working leg to rotate and move behind the shoulder. During these adjustments, use the supporting side to resist the rotation of the working leg, not the supporting hand.

When circling en dedans, adjust the torso so that the leg is able to extend and rotate to the back and then bring the body upright as the foot pushes away from the center line. To maintain the shape of the foot, push away with only the inside of the ball of the foot and the inside of the big toe.

Point

> Begin in fifth position with the arm in low fifth. Prepare the arm to second position. Use a triple-meter. Push off (1)/circle to the back (&)/through first (a). Repeat 3 times, close fifth position back on the fourth count. Reverse and repeat all.

Preparation for rond de jambe à terre

Begin in fifth position with the arm in low fifth. On the third count of a four-count preparation, battement tendu quatrième devant en fondu bringing the arm to middle fifth and inclining the head to the barre (position C), eyes focused into the palm (3), straighten the supporting knee and demi-rond de jambe à la seconde, opening the arm to second position and bringing the head erect, eyes front (4).

Correct   *Incorrect*

Make sure the inclination of the head does not affect the alignment of the shoulders or the position of the arm. Keep the shoulders level and the fingertips on the outside of the center line.

The traditional preparation of the rond de jambe à terre has its drawbacks. The ball of the foot is unable to assist the rotation of the working leg because the foot is pointed and because the position of the working leg à la seconde is static. To avoid this problem, begin the rond de jambe from fifth position front or finish the traditional preparation pointe tendue quatrième derrière.

Battement fondu à la seconde, using the arm

Coordinating the arm and leg during a battement fondu à la seconde is somewhat difficult. The arm moves through three positions and the leg moves through two yet both begin and end at the same time. Solving this problem involves learning how to control the fondu so that the arm is able to catch up with the leg.

First, practice the timing of the arm. Standing in fifth position, prepare the arm from low fifth to second position. Inhale and extend the arm through second postion (&) arrive in low fifth (1), lift the arm to middle fifth (&), open to second (2).

Next, practice the timing of the legs. Roll the working foot off the floor to point en l'air (&), fondu sur le cou-de-pied devant (1), move the working leg through attitude à la seconde (&), extend à la seconde, straightening both knees at the same time (2).

Finally, put the arm together with the legs. Roll the foot off the floor to point en l'air as the arm extends through second position (&), fondu sur le cou-de-pied devant, bringing the arm to low fifth (1), move the working leg through attitude and the arm through middle fifth (&), and open the arm to second position as both knees straighten at the same time (2). Feel as if the knees straighten because the elbow opens to the side.

Introduce battement fondu quatrième devant and derrière during the following year, adding the port de bras when the class is ready, and, lastly, coordinate the A, B, C, A head positions in coordination with the arm.

Stretching with the leg on the barre
During the third year, continue to let the students stretch each other under your supervision. In addition, introduce stretches with the leg on the lower barre. Begin first with a side stretch facing the barre, add a stretch facing the leg diagonally front, and then combine the two.

1. Side stretch, facing the barre

Before the stretch begins, make sure to align the body properly. Sit the flowerpot upright, square the hips, and rotate both legs equally. Rest the hands comfortably on the barre, shoulder width apart with the head erect and the eyes focused front. Balance the body on the ball of the supporting foot, pressing into the floor to lift the weight of the body off the leg and to prevent the pelvis from sinking into the front of the supporting hip.

Begin facing the barre with the right leg on the barre. Use a slow duplemeter. Slide the working foot along the barre (1,2)/return to vertical (3,4)/demi-plié (5,6)/straighten (7)/left arm second position (8)/bend toward the leg on the barre, moving the left arm through second to high fifth (1,2)/return to vertical, arm in high fifth (3,4)/elevé (5,6)/flat (7)/hand on barre (8). Repeat.

Maintain posture, alignment, and the rotation of both legs throughout the lunge. Move the hands with the body as the leg slides on the barre and use them to help the body return upright. To create a stretch, the thighs must separate, but if the stretch is too wide, the return to vertical will be a struggle. It should look effortless.

Once the starting position is re-established over the ball of the supporting foot, execute a deep demi-plié, knee over toe, shoulders on top of square hips, book on top of the head. As the supporting knee straightens, move the arm on the supporting side away from the barre to second position in anticipation of the cambré side.

Stretching the side opposite the direction of the bend is the goal of a cambré side, standing on two legs or with one leg on the barre. Lengthen the spine out of the pelvis. Turn the palm of the working hand over and reaching from the center of the back, lead with the wrist to draw a wide arc with the arm.

As the hand nears the head, begin to bend over the ribs (the top of the flowerpot) and, at the same time, spiral the hand to complete the curve of high fifth. Pull the working arm out of the shoulder to stretch the supporting side, taking care not to distort the curve of the arm or the U-shape between neck and shoulder.

Bend directly to the side without spiraling to or away from the working leg on the barre. Turing the head to look down at the end of the arch is preferred by some, but I find that it is easier for beginners to hold the connection between the neck and the spine when the face and focus of the eyes remain front.

Make sure to maintain the weight of the body over the ball of the supporting foot throughout the cambré and the return to vertical so that the heel is free to separate from the floor to begin the elevé that follows. Introduce cambré side, bending away from the leg on the barre, during the next year.

2. Front stretch, facing the leg

A front stretch facing diagonally with one hand on the barre feels much safer to the beginning student than one facing perpendicular to the barre with nothing to hold onto for support. Because there is nothing outside the body to line up with, however, a diagonal stretch sometimes throws off alignment. Before the stretch begins, square the hips to the leg on the barre and place the shoulders over the hips.

Carry the working arm to high fifth during the preparation. Rest the supporting hand lightly on the barre so it can slide forward as the body bends forward. Stand close enough to the barre so that the elbow is able to relax.

Begin with the right leg on the barre, facing the leg, right arm in second position. Use a slow duple-meter. Carry the arm to high fifth on the last two counts of the preparation. Bend forward (1,2)/straighten (3,4)/demi-plié (5,6)/straighten (7,8)/cambré back (1,2)/straighten (3,4)/elevé (5,6)/flat (7,8). Repeat.

Initiate the forward bend with a breath that opens the chest, lifts the face, and lengthens the spine. During the hinge, keep the hips square to target those attachments that allow the leg to lift.

Maintain a flat back during the forward bend. When the maximum stretch in this position is reached, fold the body over, letting the arm come to rest on top of the lower leg. Relax and breathe at the bottom of the stretch. Never rush the moment.

To come upright, lengthen the spine to flatten the back and place the arm in front of the head in high fifth. Pull the rotated upper arm out of the shoulder to assist the elongation of the spine, holding the shoulder down to maintain the U-shape between the neck and the arm.

Correct

Incorrect

The cambré back with one leg on the barre follows the same rules as a cambré back standing on two legs. Begin by inhaling to lengthen out of the hips and then curve the spine from a point midway between the shoulder blades. Allow the head to spill over the top of the curve but without shortening the back of the neck. Remember that if the bend is exaggerated the lower spine will be compressed and balance and alignment will be compromised.

3. Combining the front and side stretch

Begin with the right leg on the barre, facing the leg, right arm in second position. Use a slow duple-meter. On the last two counts of the preparation, bring the side arm to high fifth. Bend forward (1,2)/straighten (3,4)/demi-plié (5,6)/straighten (7,8)/cambré back (1,2)/straighten (3,4)/elevé (5)/flat (6)/detourné d'adage en dedans to face and place the hands on the barre (7)/flat (8)/slide the working foot along the barre (1,2)/return to vertical (3,4)/demi-plié (5,6)/straighten (7,8)/bend toward the working leg taking the opposite arm through second to high fifth (1,2)/return to vertical (3,4)/elevé (5)/flat (6)/detourné d'adage en dehors to face the leg (7)/flat (8). Repeat.

Stand close to the barre during the stretch to the front so that the arms will not be too far from the barre when the body turns to face the barre (detourné d'adage en dedans). In addition, keep the weight of the body over the ball of the supporting foot so that the supporting heel is able to release from the floor to initiate the turn. When the body faces the leg on the barre, turn en dedans to face the barre by rotating the supporting leg. To turn en dehors to face the leg again, rotate the leg on the barre. These rules apply whether the working leg is placed on the barre, à terre, or en l'air.

4. Arabesque stretch

Third year students normally are unable to maintain correct alignment when the leg is placed on the barre behind the body. An arabesque stretch is generally left, therefore, until the intermediate level. Until then, continue hands-on stretches and practice lifting the leg from a chair or box, holding the arms in high fifth.

When the leg is supported, place the arms in middle fifth and raise them to high fifth, slightly in front of the head. Reach through both curves to support the forward shift of the torso. Spiral to resist the rotation of the working leg, but also, to align the spine in anticipation of the cambré.

Soutenu en tournant en dedans (half-turn)

The challenge of a soutenu en tournant en dedans at the barre is to execute a half-turn from fifth position demi-pointe without the legs twisting into the shape of a pretzel. The solution is to walk the step, never resting on two legs but transferring the weight of the body from one leg to another while turning from one side to another.

Begin in fifth position with the weight of the body on the ball of the back foot. From a battement tendu à la seconde en fondu, execute a battement soutenu, lifting the supporting heel to straighten the knee and to raise the pelvis so that the working leg has room to close front, fifth position demi-pointe.

Anticipating the swivel to the other side, step onto the front foot through a slightly open fifth, freeing the back leg to rotate in the hip socket and pull the body around to the other side. Once a half-turn on the right foot is completed, place the ball of the left foot on the floor in front of the right shaping one foot with two-heels. If a balance is required at this point, distribute the weight on both feet. If a demi-plié in fifth position follows, present one foot with two heels, but keep the weight on the back foot to allow the front foot to move over the footprint of fifth position before the demi-plié.

The first time the step is performed with music, give the dancers enough time to manage the weight changes.

Begin in fifth position with the right foot front, arm in low fifth. Use a slow triple-meter. Prepare the arm to second position. Battement tendu à la seconde en fondu (a-1-&)/begin to lift the supporting heel (a)/soutenu, stepping onto right foot (2-&-a)/swivel on the right foot (3-&-a)/to fifth position demi-point, left foot front (4-&-a)/move left foot over footprint (5-&-a)/demi-plié fifth position (6-&)/straighten (a-7)/hold (&-a-8-&). Repeat left foot front. Repeat all.

When ready, execute using fewer counts.

Begin in fifth position with the right foot front, arm in low fifth. Use a triple-meter. Prepare the arm to second position. Battement tendu à la seconde en fondu (a-1-&)/begin to lift the supporting heel (a)/soutenu, stepping onto right foot (2)/swivel on the right foot to fifth position demi-pointe, left foot front (a-3)/move left foot over footprint (a)/ demi-plié fifth position (4)/straighten (&). Repeat left foot in front. Repeat all.

Eventually perform the soutenu en tournant en dedans in four counts, using either a duple or triple-meter.

Begin in fifth position with the right foot front, arm in low fifth. Prepare the arm to second position. Battement tendu a la second en fondu (&-1)/ begin to lift the supporting heel (&)/soutenu, stepping and turning on right foot (2-&)/to fifth position demi-pointe, left foot front (3)/move left foot over footprint (&)/demi-plié fifth position (4)/straighten (&)/hold (5-8). Repeat left foot front. Repeat all.

Once the soutenu en tournant en dedans is mastered, use it during the last four counts of an exercise to change sides at the barre.

Piqué arabesque

Practice the pique arabesque without music, facing the barre.

Start in fifth position with the weight of the body on the ball of the back foot. Execute a dégagé en l'air quatrième devant en fondu, brushing the working foot out of fifth position as the supporting knee bends. Already visualize the shape of the back leg in arabesque as the extended foot points toward a landing spot on the floor just beyond the toes.

From the preparation, push off the ball of the supporting foot to move the body up and onto the standing spot and to lift the leg en l'air.

Get on top of the leg first before taking hold of the barre. Make sure to draw a V-shape with the torso and the working thigh, to spiral the torso away from the rotation of the working leg, and to stand securely on top of a high demi-pointe, the penthouse, before lowering both heels at the same time in fifth position demi-plié.

Once the dancers are able to successfully execute a piquè arabesque, facing the barre, practice the step moving from one end of the barre to the other, using one hand. As the body shifts forward during the piqué, remember to move the hand on the barre and the side arm, held in second position, with the body.

Let the first dancer execute the step two times before the next dancer begins so that each one has enough room to extend the leg. Each dancer should walk into fifth position and prepare the arm to second position with the music as the dancer in front takes her turn.

> Begin in fifth position with the inside foot front, arm in second position. Use a slow triple-meter. Battement dégagé en l'air quatrième devant en fondu with the inside leg (1-&-a)/piqué arabesque (2)/demi-plié fifth position (3-&)/straighten (a-4). Repeat 4 times.

In order to land on the second count in the above combination, move through the bottom of the fondu preparation and push off of the ball of the supporting foot on the second pulse (a) following the first count.

IN THE CENTER

Adage

If the class is able to maintain line and balance during développé à la seconde and quatrième devant at the barre, incorporate these steps into an adage performed in the center. Continue to lift the leg to an arabesque from tendu quatrième derrière. Wait until the fourth year, when the dancers are stronger, to introduce a développé in that direction.

> Begin in fifth position with the right foot front, arms in low fifth. Use a slow duple-meter. Retiré devant, arms middle fifth (&-1,2)/extend attitude à la seconde, arms second position (3,4)/extend à la seconde (5)/fifth position back (&-6)/ lengthen arms (7)/bend the elbows to return the arms to low fifth (&-8). Repeat to the other side.

In the above exercise, substitute développé à la seconde with a développé quatrième devant. To change legs, execute a battement tendu à la seconde at the same time the arms lengthen. Close fifth back as the arms return to low fifth.

When standing on one leg, it is especially important to use the rotation of the upper arm on the supporting side to balance the actions occurring on the working side. Rotation creates an upward pressure that can be used to secure balance should the flowerpot begin to tilt.

By the end of the third year, if the class is ready, enrich the adage by including diagonal extensions, varying the position of the arms, and changing directions by means of a pas de bourreé or glissade.

> Begin in fifth position with the right foot front, effacé devant, arms in low fifth, head turned and inclined. Use a slow duple-meter. Battement tendu effacé devant, arms high third, left arm high and right arm side (&-1)/ dégagé en l'air effacé devant (&-2) pointe tendue effacé devant (&-3)/fifth position (&-4)/battement tendu effacé derrière (&-5)/fondu en arabesque (6)/pas de bourrée dessous to demi-plié fifth position effacé devant, left foot front, circling the arms outside to low fifth (&-a-7)/straighten, head turned and inclined (8). Repeat to the other side.

> Begin in fifth position with the right foot front, croisé devant, arms in low fifth, head turned and inclined. Use a slow triple-meter. Battement tendu croisé devant, arms high third, right arm high and left arm side (a-1-&)/ dégagé en l'air (a-2-&)/pointe tendue croisé devant (a-3-&) fifth position (a-4)/battement tendu écarté devant (a-5-&)/ dégagé en l'air (a-6-&)/fondu cou-de-pied derrière, place high arm in second (a-7)/pas de bourrée dessous

to demi-plié fifth position effacé devant, right foot front, moving the arms through second to low fifth (&-a-8)/straighten to battement tendu effacé derrière, left arm in high third and right arm side (a-1-&)/dégagé en l'air (a-2-&)/pointe tendue effacé derrière (a-3-&)/pass through first position to croisé devant (a-4)/dégagé en fondu (5-&) piqué fifth position demi-pointe (a-6)/demi-plié fifth, right arm to high fifth (7-&)/straighten and circle the arms away from the body (a)/ low fifth, head inclined (8). Repeat to the other side.

Arabesque

During the first year of training, students learn to identify and imitate the first three arabesques and how to execute a battement tendu quatrième derrière.

During the second year, battement dégagé quatrième derrière and dégagé en l'air quatrième derrière are introduced at the barre, and, eventually, an arabesque en l'air, lifting from pointe tendue quatrième derrière, is incorporated into an adage in the center. The students also spend time refining the shape of the arms in each position, learning how they connect within the back and how they relate to other parts of the body.

During the third year at the barre, second arabesque à terre is incorporated into battement tendu en croix. Students learn how to extend the leg to the back from the ankle and the knee and how to bend the working leg as the supporting leg lifts. They practice lifting the leg off a support while shaping the arms in high fifth and learn how to execute a piqué arabesque at the barre. In the center, dégagés en l'air and en fondu are performed diagonally in the center with the arms in either high third, high fifth, or first arabesque. First and second arabesque continue to be practiced à terre and en l'air, with and without support for the leg, anticipating the detourné and the promenade.

Listed below is a summation of the various actions and reactions that help to achieve technical and artistic clarity when the leg is held in the arabesque position.

1. Shift the torso forward so that the leg is able to extend and lift to the back.
2. Rotate the working leg fully, allowing the working hip to open slightly.
3. Scoop the abdominal muscles and press into the floor through the ball of the supporting foot to balance the stretch of the extended leg.
4. Rotate the supporting leg to balance the rotation of the working leg.
5. Spiral the upper body in opposition to the rotation of the working leg.
6. Keep the sides parallel and the shoulders level as the working leg lifts.
7. When applicable, use the rotation of the upper arms to stabilize the balance.
8. Balance the stretch of the leg extended to the back by stretching the arm or arms extended to the front.

9. Stretch one arm to equal the stretch of the other arm.

10. Pull the shoulders down in response to the upward scoop of the abdominal muscles and the rotation of the upper arms.

11. Close the ribs as the chin lifts.

Notice how one part of the body works off another, like two teams in a game of tug of war.

3 Transition steps

Pas de bourrée dessus

A pas de bourrée is considered dessus when the working leg starts either fifth front or fifth back and moves over or on top of the supporting leg to shape fifth position demi-pointe.

> Begin in fifth position with the right foot back, arms in low fifth. Use a duple-meter. Battement dégagé à la seconde en fondu with the right leg (&-1)/begin to lift the supporting heel (&) soutenu to fifth position demi-pointe, right foot in front (2)/step onto the left foot pointing the right foot (3)/demi-plié fifth position right foot back (4)/three changement (&-5)/ (&-6)/(&-7)/straighten (8). Repeat to the other side. Repeat all.

Since the class is already proficient in the performance of the pas de bourreé dessous, the pas de bourrée dessus may be introduced in the center.

Temps lié à la seconde

While a glissade and a pas de bourrée move the body through an upward arc from one place to another, temps lié à la seconde, meaning linking step, moves the body in a downward arc, sliding through a demi-plié in second.

> Begin in fifth position with the right foot front, arms in low fifth. Use a triple-meter. Prepare the arms to second position. Demi-plié (1-&)/temps lié à la seconde (a-2)/fifth position, left foot front (a-3)/hold (&-a-4-&-a). Repeat to the other side. Repeat all.

Support the weight of the body over the over the ball of the back leg, standing in fifth and during the demi-plié, so that the front foot is free to slide sideways through demi-plié second position. At the end of the slide, push away from the floor with the ball of the supporting foot to complete the shift of weight onto the right leg. Because the left leg begins behind the right in the starting fifth position, move it forward slightly to shape à la seconde, heel in front of foot, as both knees straighten. Keep the knees aligned over the toes and balance the flowerpot on the table from the beginning of the temps lié to the end. Increase the rotation of the upper right arm slightly to help the right side resist the force of the body as it moves sideways.

> Begin in fifth position with the right foot front, arms in low fifth. Use a triple-meter. Prepare the arms to second position. Demi-plié fifth position (1-&)/temps lié à la seconde in the direction of the front foot, taking the

arms from second position to high fifth as the left leg reaches tendu à la seconde (a–2)/demi-plié fifth position, left foot front, moving the arms from high fifth to middle fifth (3–&)/straighten the knees and open the arms to second position (a–4). Repeat to the other side. Repeat all.

Temps lié quatrième en avant and en arrière.

Like a temps lié à la seconde, temps lié en avant and en arrière begin with the weight of the body on the ball of the supporting leg both in fifth position and during the preparatory demi-plié. Moving to the front, slide the front foot out of fifth and with the ball of the back foot, push the body forward and on top of the front leg. Moving to the back, slide the back foot out of fifth and with the ball of the front foot, push the body back on top of the back leg.

No matter the direction of the step, keep the knees supple so that the body is able to slide through a deep demi-plié. At the same time, rotate the upper arms to lift the body off the legs. Hold the body upright, head erect and shoulders on top of the hips, with one exception. When the leg extends to the back, shift the torso forward. Remember to hold the ribs together to prevent the back from arching and to spiral the upper body to resist the rotation of the back leg.

Begin in fifth position with the right foot front, arms in low fifth. Use a triple-meter. Prepare the arms to second position. Demi-plié (1–&)/temps lié quatrième en avant to pointe tendue quatrième derrière (a–2)/fondu sur le cou-de-pied derrière (3)/pas de bourrée dessous (&–a) fifth position demi-plié (4–&)/straighten (a)/demi-plié fifth position (5–&)/temps lié à la seconde to the right in the direction of the back foot (a–6)/fondu sur le cou de pied derrière (7)/pas de bourrée dessous (&–a)/demi-plié fifth position, left foot front (8–&)/straighten (a). Repeat to the other side. Repeat all.

Chassé en diagonal

During the first and second years, consecutive chassés traveling en avant are performed diagonally across the floor. Throughout the second year and continuing into the third, as the class learns some specific detail that will improve the chassé, new knowledge is applied to the old step.

Remember that the slide-together of the chassé should not be confused with the step-together of the gallop. A gallop is a connecting step that leads into a tour jeté, a temps levé en arabesque, or a saut de basque.

During the third year, take time to focus specifically on the end position of the chassé, effacé derrière en fondu with the arms in high third. Face the body toward the front corner of a square, with the downstage arm rounded overhead and the other arm placed to the side. Keep the head in line with the spine and rotate it toward the mirror. If the arm hides the face, do not drop the chin down. Instead, stretch the upper arm back in the shoulder.

While it is acceptable to incline the turned head toward the back, it is easier for beginning students to hold the head in line with the spine. This position is more in sync with the tilt of the body and the direction of the movement. Make sure, however, that the head turns to the side on top of the neck, not from the waist.

Next, stand in fifth position, right foot effacé devant, arms in high third. Remember, the starting position of the feet predicts the direction of a movement. Face the body so that the inside of the heel of the back foot can be seen by the audience.

From fifth position, execute a demi-plié and practice sliding through a demi-plié in fourth position to finish pointe tendue effacé derrière en fondu. Pose en fondu to feel if the body is still facing the front corner of the square, if the back leg is extended behind the same shoulder, and if the spiral of the upper body is resisting the turn of the head and the rotation of the leg. Feel if the flowerpot is upright and if the supporting knee is directed over the toes of the supporting foot.

When the end position can be presented clearly, put the parts of the chassé back together. Start from fifth position effacé devant with the weight over the ball of the back foot and the arms in high third. Execute a demi-plié and, using the back foot, push the body through fourth position onto the ball of the front foot. Once the weight shifts, spring off the front foot, bringing the body upright and lifting the hips straight up into the air to make room for the legs to kiss, fifth position en l'air. Returning to fifth position demi-plié, catch the weight of the body on the back foot, ready to slide out of fifth into the next chassé. Maintain the height of the chin and the rotation of the back leg throughout.

When the class is ready, perform a series of chassés across the floor with music. Start from the upstage corner, allowing four counts to go by before the next individual or group begins. Keep facing the front corner of the square as the square moves diagonally downstage.

> Begin in fifth position with the right foot front, effacé devant, arms in low fifth. Use a quick triple-meter. Prepare the arms through middle fifth on the second count of a four-count preparation, to high third on the third count, and demi-plié on the fourth count. Slide (1)/spring (&)/land (a)/slide (2).

Note that the step is performed in a single count divided into three pulses (1-&-a), one pulse for the slide, one for fifth position en l'air, and one for the landing. Whether the chassé begins with a spring or a slide, execute the slide on the count. Use sounds, such as shump-pa-pa, to describe the contrasting qualities of the movement and lower the pitch of your voice to emphasize the depth of the slide.

When the shape of the chassé can be maintained moving across the floor, combine with other steps that can be used to change the direction of the body.

> Begin in fifth position with the right foot front, effacé devant, arms in low fifth. Use a duple-meter. Demi-plié on the last count of the preparation. Sauté fifth position en l'air, arms middle fifth (&)/demi-plié fifth, weight on the back foot (a)/slide through fifth, effacé en avant and point effacé derrière, arms to high third, left arm high (1)/pas de bourrée circling both arms around (&-a)/demi-plié, arms low fifth (2)/changement (&-3)/changement changing direction to effacé devant, left foot front (&-4). Repeat to the other side. Repeat all.

Chassé quatrième en avant

Practice chassé en avant, with the arms in second position and the eyes focused to the front. Travelling forward, it will be easy to see if the spiral of the upper body and the direction of the leg are correct, but it will still be necessary to feel those things that can't be seen. Hold the ribs together and maintain the relationship of the arms to the shoulders as the body moves forward through space, and make sure that the back leg does not lose rotation when it moves between fifth position demi-plié and fifth position en l'air.

Add a port de bras when the class is ready.

Begin in fifth position with the right foot front, arms in low fifth. Use a quick triple-meter. Demi-plié on the last count of the preparation. Sauté to fifth position in the air, arms middle fifth (&)/demi-plié fifth position, weight on the back foot (a)/slide quatrième en avant, open arms to second position (1)/pas de bourrée dessous, arms through second to low fifth (&-a-2). Repeat to the other side. Repeat all.

When the class begins to practice pirouettes en dehors from fourth position, use the above exercise to move into a preparatory fourth position after the pas de bourrée.

Sissonne tombée

It is possible to break down sissone tombée facing the mirror, but if the class is already working on a diagonal, introduce the step travelling effacé en avant, changing sides by means of a pas de bourreé dessous.

To practice the step, place the hands on the shoulders, elbows extended side.

Begin in fifth position with the right foot front, effacé devant, hands on shoulders. Use a slow duple-meter. Demi-plié on the last count of the preparation. Sauté to fifth position en l'air (&)/land on the back foot en fondu, extending the right leg effacé devant (a)/tombée efface en avant, extending the left leg effacé derrière (1)/pas de bourrée dessous to demi-plié fifth position effacé devant, facing left with the left foot front (&-a-2). Repeat to the other side. Repeat all 4 times.

Begin in fifth position with the right foot front, croisé devant, hands on the shoulders. Use a slow duple-meter. Demi-plié on the last count of the preparation. Sauté to fifth position en l'air to face right, effacé devant (&)/land on the back foot en fondu, extending the right leg effacé devant (a)/tombée onto the right leg, extending the left leg effacé derrière (1)/pas de bourrée dessous to demi-plié fifth position croisé devant with the left foot front (&-a-2). Repeat to the other side. Repeat all 4 times.

It is easy to overshoot a diagonal when changing directions in the air. Work within the square, ignoring the strong pull of the real corners and walls of the existing room. Be aware specifically of the placement of the supporting foot at the end of the sissonne since it determines the direction of the tombée.

Add a port de bra to the sissonne tombée pas de bourrée dessous once the class is able to direct the body properly and maintain the shape of the legs when changing directions. Begin with the arms in low fifth. Move to middle fifth on the spring, hold middle fifth on the landing, open to second position on the tombée, extend through second position on the pas de bourrée, and return to low fifth during the demi-plié fifth position. Or begin with the arms in low fifth. Move to middle fifth on the spring, hold middle fifth on the landing, open to high third on the tombée, and circle to the outside of the body to low fifth during the pas de bourrée dessous to fifth position demi-plié.

Remember, any action of the body has an opposite and equal reaction. If something pulls one way, something else pulls the other way. If something spirals one way, something else spirals the other way. Ask the class how many opposites they can find in a sissonne tombée.

Balancé de côté

Practicing triplets the first two years prepares for the balancé introduced during the third year. Place the arms on the shoulders while learning how to move the legs and feet.

From a demi-plié in fifth position, right foot back, execute a low développé à la seconde passing the right foot by the back of the ankle. Allow the elongation of the working leg to pull the body off balance onto the right leg and as soon as the weight shifts, drag the left foot, without pointing, under the right foot. Step onto the ball of the left foot and return immediately to the right foot, like the tap step, ball/change, shaping a diamond with the legs. Repeat the balancé to the other side by executing a développé with the left leg to pull the body off balance again, this time to the left. Make sure the foot points at the end of each développé.

Perform with music once the students are able to shape each part of the step correctly. Until then, count the meter.

Begin in fifth position with the right foot back, hands on the shoulders, elbows pointed to the side. Use a slow triple-meter. Demi-plié on the last count of the preparation. Développé à la seconde (a)/tombée right (1)/step under left (&)/step right and développé left (a).

During the weight change, many teachers require the dancers to straighten the knees, reach a full demi-point, and shape one foot sur le cou-de-pied. For the purpose of achieving a more fluid movement, one without an accent, I prefer that students maintain a demi-plié throughout the step, keeping the knees supple with just a subtle rise and fall of the body. Move into the floor rather than on top of it. Feel as if you are dancing on a sponge cake.

Eventually add a movement of the arms. Prepare the arms to second position and during the step, round the left arm in front when moving to the right

and round the right arm moving to the left. Feel as if the arms are moving side to side through the weight of water. Allow the hand of the arm in second position to trail a little before folding into middle third.

Turn and incline the head on top of the neck in the direction of the rounded arm and focus over the forearm. As students advance they will learn how to spiral the upper body in the direction of the tombée and in opposition to the inclination of the head and the rotation of the back leg.

Begin in fifth position with the right foot back, arms in low fifth. Use a triple-meter. Prepare the arms to second position. Balancé right and left six times changing arms (1–6)/step right, arms second position (7–&–a)/close fifth back (8). Repeat to the other side. Repeat all.

Practice the above combination in straight lines, one line at a time.

Soutenu en tournant en dedans

> Begin in fifth position with the right foot front, arms in low fifth. Use a triple-meter. Prepare the arms to second position. Battement tendu à la seconde en fondu with the right leg (a–1)/soutenu, turning left to face the side wall, finishing fifth position demi-pointe, right foot front, arms middle fifth (a–2)/demi-plié fifth position (3–&)/straighten and open arms to second position (a–4). Repeat 3 more times facing each wall until a full turn has been completed or alternate legs to return to the front. Repeat.

From battement tendu à la seconde en fondu, release the supporting heel and push away from the floor to spring. Use the force of the arms, moving from second to middle fifth, the rotation of the supporting leg, and the energy of the relevé to turn the body as it leaves the floor. Spring and turn at the same time, keeping the torso upright and moving the working leg with the hip, as if executing a pirouette à la seconde en dedans. Arrive on both feet at the same time, fifth position demi-pointe, facing the side wall. Move the front foot over the footprint of fifth position and demi-plié.

When quarter turns become secure, practice half-turns.

> Begin in fifth position with the right foot back, arms in low fifth. Use a triple-meter. Prepare the arms to second position. Battement tendu à la seconde en fondu with the right leg (a–1)/relevé, turning left en dedans to face the back wall, fifth position demi-pointe, right foot front, arms middle fifth (a–2)/demi-plié fifth position (3–&)/straighten and open arms to second position (a–4). Reverse, extending the left leg to second from fifth position, turning right en dedans and, finishing fifth position demi-pointe, left foot front. Repeat all.

Once students are able to complete a half-turn to face the back, add a final swivel turn, demi-detourné en dehors, to bring the body back to the front. Remember that the legs are able to swivel no more than a half-turn, which means the initial relevé, by necessity, must also complete a half-turn.

> Begin in fifth position with the right foot back, arms in low fifth. Use a triple-meter. Prepare the arms to second position. Battement tendu à la seconde en fondu with the right leg (a–1)/relevé, turning left en dedans to face the back wall, fifth position demi-pointe, right foot front, arms middle fifth (a–2)/swivel on right foot (a)/to face front, fifth position demi-pointe (3)/find footprint (a)/demi-plié (4)/straighten (&). Hold four counts before repeating. Repeat 4 times.

When the body faces the back wall, fifth position demi-pointe, support the weight of the body on the front foot as the front leg continues to rotate to the right, use the rotation of the back leg to turn the body left. At the end of the swivel turn place the left foot in fifth position demi-pointe, shaping one foot with two heels. No bourrées allowed! From demi-pointe, move the front foot over the footprint of fifth position, demi-plié, and straighten the knees ready to repeat the soutenu in the same direction.

Note that the soutenu en tournant, like a pas de bourrée, is a walking step. Prepare, rise, and turn and on the left foot to face the back wall, step and swivel on the right foot to face front, and stop by stepping onto the left foot.

To execute a soutenu en tournant from fifth position, begin with the right foot front, demi-plié, and spring to face the back wall, landing on the balls of the feet, fifth position demi-point, right foot front. From there, demi-detourné en dehors to face front and finish demi-plié fifth position.

To withstand the power of the relevé and to sustain the verticality as the body turns, keep the ribs closed, upper arms rotated, eyes focused on the horizon, and maintain a high demi-pointe, pushing away from the floor until the knees begin to bend at the end of step.

Detourné d'adage à terre en dedans and en dehors

The students became familiar with detourné d'adage en dedans and en dehors when they learned to change from one direction to another with the leg on the barre. To review, a detourné d'adage is a slow, controlled pivot on one leg that turns the body a quarter turn at the same time the working leg changes position. It is said to turn en dedans when the body turns in the direction of the supporting leg and en dehors when the body turns in the direction of the working leg.

Start with the least difficult directional change, moving from battement tendu quatrième devant, facing front, to battement tendu à la seconde, facing the wall.

Begin in fifth position with the right foot front, arms in low fifth. Use a slow triple-meter. Prepare the arms to second position. Battement tendu quatrième devant (a–1)/detourné d'adage à terre en dedans (a)/à la seconde, facing the side wall (2)/close fifth front (a–3)/hold (&–a–4–&). Repeat 4 times to complete a half-turn. Repeat all.

In the above combination, release the supporting heel on the pulse (a) that follows the count (1), allowing the supporting leg to rotate and turn the body. At the same time, rotate the working leg in the opposite direction as it moves à la seconde, heel in front of foot. At the end of the step, touch the floor with the supporting heel and the working toe on the same count (2).

Perform the detourné in coordination with the breath. Inhale to lift the heel and exhale to lower it. Scoop the abdominals to lighten the weight held on top of the supporting leg and, whenever necessary, increase the rotation of one or both of the upper arms to balance the body. As the body pivots, make sure the arms move with the shoulders.

Next, reverse the direction of the detourné discussed above. Begin à la seconde and move en dehors to quatrième devant.

With both legs rotated equally, this time release the supporting heel to allow the rotation of the working leg to turn the body. At the end of the pivot, line up the working leg with the shoulder as the toes of the working foot touch the floor at the same time as the supporting heel.

The most difficult version of the detourné d'adage à terre moves en dedans from à la seconde to quatrième derrière. The challenge is to maintain the rotation and stretch of the

working leg as it moves behind the body and lines up with the shoulder, even as the rotation of the supporting leg, the spiral of the upper body, core strength, and the connective energies of the arms all work together to shift the body in the opposite direction, up and forward.

Changing from battement tendu quatrième derrière to à la seconde is not so difficult. Initiate the turn by rotating the back leg and bring the body upright.

Combine two or more directions once the detourné d'adage is mastered.

> Begin in fifth position with the right foot in front, arms in low fifth. Use a slow triple-meter. Prepare the arms to second position. Battement tendu quatrième devant (a–1)/detourné d'adage à terre en dedans à la seconde (a–2)/detourné d'adage à terre en dehors quatrième devant (a–3/close fifth (a–4). Repeat 4 times.

To the above combination, add a battement tendu quatrième derrière (a–5)/detourné d'adage à terre en dehors à la seconde (a–6)/detourné d'adage à terre en dedans to quatrième derrière (a–7)/close fifth (a–8).

Next, combine three directions to complete a half-turn.

> Begin in fifth position with the right foot front, arms in low fifth. Use a triple-meter. Prepare the arms to second position. Battement tendu quatrième devant (a–1)/hold (&–a–2–&)/detourné d'adage à terre en dedans à la seconde (a–3)/hold (&–a–4–&)/detourné d'adage à terre en dedans to tendu quatrième derrière (a–5)/hold (&–a–6–&)/close fifth position (a–7)/hold (&–a–8–&). Reverse, turning en dehors. Repeat all.

Add a final level of complexity by changing the arms from second position to first arabesque as the working leg moves from the side to the back and the body moves from the front to the side.

Practice the changes of the upper body first. Begin facing front with the arms in second position and visualize the shape of first arabesque. Next, take tiny steps to change directions and, at the same time, turn the palms over to form two straight lines, one arm extending front from one shoulder and the other arm extending side and a little behind the other shoulder. Stretch both arms with equal energy but without locking the elbows.

Moving from first arabesque to shape the long curves of second position, rotate the upper arms, releasing the elbows, and bring the palms to face the front.

Put the movements of the upper body together with the movements of the lower body when the students are ready.

Begin in fifth position with the right foot front, arms in low fifth. Use a slow triple-meter. Prepare the arms to second position. Battement tendu à la seconde with the right foot (a-1)/detourné d'adage à terre en dedans to first arabesque left arm front, right arm side (a-2)/detourné d'adage à terre en dehors à la seconde, returning the arms to second position (a-3)/close fifth position, right foot back (a-4). Repeat to the other side. Repeat all.

Begin in fifth position with the right foot front, arms in low fifth. Use a slow triple-meter. Prepare the arms to second position. Battement tendu à la seconde with the right foot (a-1)/detourné d'adage à terre en dedans to first arabesque, left arm front and right arm side (a-2)/detourné d'adage à terre en dehors à la seconde, arms second position (a-3)/close fifth position, right foot front (a-4-&,a-5-&)/demi-plié, rounding the right arm to middle fifth (a)/ pirouette (6-&-a)/demi-plié, right foot back, arms middle fifth (7-&)/straighten (a)/and prepare the arms to second position (8). Repeat to the other side. Repeat all.

Detourné d'adage en l'air

Once the class is able to maintain balance, rotation, and alignment, holding the leg 45 degrees in all directions, and is able to perform a detourné d'adage à terre clearly and securely, proceed to the detourné d'adage en l'air. Save for the intermediate level if the class is not yet strong enough.

The detouné d'adage en l'air follows the same principles as the detourné d'adage à terre. The rotation of either the working or supporting leg initiates a quarter turn and, at the same time, the working leg changes position.

Begin in fifth position with the right foot front, arms in low fifth. Use a slow triple-meter. Prepare the arms to second position. Battement tendu à la seconde with the right leg (a-1)/dégagé en l'air (2)/detourné d'adage en dedans to first arabesque left arm front, right arm side (&-3)/fondu arabesque (4)/pas de bourrée dessous to demi-plié fifth position bringing arms to and through second to low fifth (&-a-5)/glissade change to the right (&-6)/straighten both knees, bringing arms to middle fifth (7)/open arms to second position (8). Repeat to the other side. Repeat all.

To help a student understand how to shift the torso while making the transition from à la seconde to first arabesque, stand to her supporting side and take hold of her hand. Lend light support as the heel lifts and then pull her gently toward you as she sets it down.

Begin in fifth position with the right foot front, arms in low fifth. Use a triple-meter. Prepare the arms to second position. Battement tendu à la seconde with the right leg (a-1-&)/dégagé en l'air (a-2-&)/detourné d'adage en dedans (a) to first arabesque left arm front, right arm side (3-&,a-4-&)/detourné d'adage en dehors (a)/à la seconde, returning arms to second position (5-&,a-6-&)/pointe tendue à la seconde (a-7-&)/close fifth position, right foot back (a-8). Repeat to the other side. Repeat all.

Begin in fifth position with the right foot front, arms in low fifth. Use a triple-meter. Prepare the arms to middle fifth on the second count of a four-count preparation, extend through second position on the third count, and return them to low fifth on the fourth count. Retiré devant, moving arms to middle fifth (1-&-a,2-&-a)/développé à la seconde, opening arms to second position (3-&-a,4-&)/detourné d'adage en dedans to first arabesque, left arm front and right arm side (a-5)/fondu arabesque (6)/pas de bourrée dessus to demi-plié fifth position, passing the arms to and through second position to low fifth (&-a-7-&), straighten (a-8). Repeat to the other side. Repeat all.

In the above exercise, face front and change the arms to second position at the end of the soutenu that begins the pas de bourrée. Move the arms through second position on the side step of the pas de bourrée and bend the elbows as the knees bend to lower the heels to fifth position demi-plié.

En promenade

When a position is supported on one leg and turned slowly from one point to another by moving the heel, it is said to be en promenade, "in a walk." Like a figure on top of a music box, the slow turn shows the body from all angles. While arabesque and attitude are most commonly displayed en promenade, retiré devant, with the arms in middle fifth, is a more practical position for beginners. It is easier to turn when the arms and legs are held close to the body and, because a pivot in this position mimics a pirouette in slow motion, the dancers learn specifically how the legs, the arms, the sides, and the focus of the eyes function to balance and turn the body around.

With the weight of the body on the ball of the supporting foot, lift and shift the supporting heel to turn the body. To make sure the promenade is smooth, cover an equal amount of space and lift the heel the same height during each shift. To make sure the promenade is musical, use an equal amount of time for each shift. For instance, if a half-turn is accompanied by a duple-meter, make four equal shifts, one shift per count. If a full turn must be completed in the same amount of time, move the heel on both the count and the pulse of that count.

Initiate the promenade by rotating the working or supporting leg depending on the direction of the turn. If the right leg is placed retiré devant, use the right thigh to turn to the right, en dehors. To turn the body to the left, en dedans, use the rotation of the supporting leg.

Pivot the body without losing the shape of the position. Keep the focus even, shoulders level, the flowerpot upright, upper arms rotated, and both legs rotated equally. Scoop the abdominals and press through the ball of the supporting foot, shape the working foot, touching the little toenail lightly at the supporting knee, and move the supporting heel without bending the supporting knee.

> Begin in fifth position with the right foot front, arms in low fifth. Use a slow duple-meter. Lift the arms to middle fifth on the last count of the preparation. Lift heel (&)/point sur le cou-de-pied devant (1) retiré devant (2)/shift four times en dehors to face the back wall (3,4,5,6)/lower right leg to fifth position (7,8). Repeat, turning in the same direction to return to the front. Repeat all.

Next, reverse the above exercise. With the right foot retiré devant, promenade to the left, en dedans, using the rotation of the supporting leg to turn the body. When ready, introduce a promenade in arabesque, making a half-turn.

> Begin in fifth position with the right foot front, effacé devant, arms in low fifth. Use a triple-meter. Demi-plié fifth position, arms middle fifth (1)/ temps lie efface en avant, sweeping the arms through low fifth, finishing tendu effacé derrière, arms in first arabesque (&-a-2)/dégagé en l'air (3,4)/shift two times to face the right back corner (5,6)/arabesque fondue (7)/pas de bourrée dessous turning en dehors (&-a) demi-plié fifth position, left foot front, effacé devant (8)/straighten (&). Repeat to the other side. Repeat all.

The above exercise may also be done beginning in fifth position right foot croisé devant.

> Demi-plié fifth position, arms to middle fifth (1)/temps lie croisé en avant, sweeping the arms through low fifth (&-a) tendu croisé derrière, right arm front and left arm side (2-&-a)/dégagé en l'air (3,4)/ shift two times to face the right front corner in first arabesque (5,6)/ arabesque fondue (7)/pas de bourrée dessus, arms through second position (&-a) demi-plié fifth position left foot croisé devant, arms to low fifth (8)/straighten knees (&). Repeat to the other side. Repeat all.

In the preparatory fifth of the previous combination, make sure the body faces the corner of the square with the inside of the front heel visible to the audience. If the heel cannot be seen, sharpen the diagonal, facing the body more to the front.

During the promenade, maintain the shape of the position and the height of the leg.

Begin in fifth position with the right foot front, croisé devant, arms in low fifth. Use a slow triple-meter. Retiré devant, arms to middle fifth (1,2)/ développé croisé devant, arms high third, right arm high and left arm side (3,4)/ demi-grand rond de jambe en l'air to écarté devant (5,6)/fondu sur le cou-de-pied derrière (7)/pas de bourrée dessous (&-a) to demi-plié fifth position effacé, right foot front, arms middle fifth (8)/temps lié effacé en avant, arm through low fifth (&)/to pointe tendue effacé derrière, arms in first arabesque (1)/dégagé en l'air (2)/promenade to back corner (3,4)/ arabesque fondue (5)/pas de bourrée dessous en dehors, arms to and through second position (&-a)/to demi-plié fifth position croisé, left foot front, arms in low fifth (6)/soussous arms to high fifth (7), demi-plié fifth position arms to low fifth (8)/straighten (&). Repeat to the other side.

Chaînés turns, using the arms

During the third year, continue to refine the shape and musicality of chaînés turns and begin using the arms. The arms, combined with the preparatory spring and the action of spotting, provide momentum for the series of turns.

Start in the upstage left corner, standing in fifth position croisé devant, right foot front, and pointe tendue croisé devant, arms in middle third, right arm rounded. Execute a dégagé en fondu on the last count (8) of the preparation, push off the ball of the supporting foot on the following pulse (&), and land on the extended leg on the first count (1) of the exercise.

Open the right arm to turn right on the right leg and close the left arm to turn right on the left leg. In second position, be careful that the arms do not open beyond the shoulders. In middle fifth, keep the hands lower than the

Once a new skill is learned and perfected, incorporate it into an adage when appropriate. Use transition steps such glissade, soutenu, and relevé passé to change the feet or the direction. Use demi-grand rond de jambe en l'air, detourné en l'air and promenades as well as développés to build strength. Add port de bras and cambrés to rest the muscles. Create an adage that travels diagonally across the room by combining a chassé pas de bourrée or a tombé pas de bourrée with a pirouette. Finish with chainée turns or simply an elegant walk.

elbows and reach with the fingers to shape, but not to complete, the circle. In both positions, rotate the upper arms to assist balance.

Rotate both legs equally from start to finish. Use the rotation of the right leg to turn the body right and pull the left leg along as it continues to rotate left.

Use a duple-meter, making sure that each step on the diagonal corresponds to an equal division of musical time, (1,&,2,&,3,&,4,&). Keep the legs directly underneath the shoulders during the turns and maintain a consistently high demi-pointe.

As the class advances and the tempo of the music increases, narrow the space between the heels. In addition, open and close the arms only a few turns to build momentum and then hold them in middle fifth until the series is completed.

Piqué turn en dedans

Before introducing a series of piqué turns en dedans across the floor, the students should be able to execute a well-balanced piqué retiré derrière without the barre.

Begin in the upstage left corner, standing in fifth position croisé devant right foot front. Pointe tendue croisé devant with the arms in middle third, right arm rounded, and look toward the downstage corner. Use a triple-meter so that the dancers are challenged to balance long enough to complete a full turn. Execute a dégagé en fondu on the pulse (&) following the last count of the preparation (8) and, keeping the body upright and the supporting thigh rotated, spring onto the right leg on the first count (1) of the exercise. As the ball of the left foot pushes away from the floor, open the right leg over the diagonal extended to the upstage corner.

Remember to leave the floor slightly when transferring from one leg to another. If a student has a habit of putting the extended leg on the floor before the supporting leg has a chance to push away from the floor, try this experiment. Eliminate the turn and execute a simple piqué retiré onto a thin book placed on the floor. By raising the floor, the dancer will instinctively use more force to spring. Falling onto the extended leg will no longer be an option.

Use the energy from the spring not only to turn the body but to direct the inside of the heel to the back of the knee. Place the heel as high as it can go without displacing the hips. Shape retiré derrière, a triangle, by rotating the thigh in opposition to the direction of the turn.

Along with the spring, use the arms to help turn the body. Open the right arm with the working leg as it moves over the diagonal during the spring and close the left arm to middle fifth as the weight transfers onto that leg. In both positions, rotate the upper arms, keeping the elbows lower than the shoulders and the hands lower than the elbows. In middle fifth, reach through the fingers toward the midline.

Use the head to help complete the turn. Focus toward the downstage right corner as long as the head is able to remain erect and then whip the head around to look to the corner once again, pulling the body around after it.

To return to the starting position, coupé (see page 172) with the left foot and extend the right leg croisé devant as the left arm opens to the side. Continue to look toward the right corner even as the turn finishes with the body facing to the left.

Control the descent of the heel during the coupé. If the body falls into or sits in the coupé, the power of the recoil will be lost.

> Begin in the upstage left corner, fifth position croise devant, right foot front, arms in low fifth. Prepare the right leg tendu croisé devant and round the right arm to middle third on the last count of the preparation. Dégagé croisé devant en fondu (a)/piqué turn bringing both arms to middle fifth (1-&)/ coupe dégagé croisé devant en fondu, returning the arms to middle third (a). Continue downstage on a diagonal.

Pirouette en dedans from fourth position

The following exercise prepares for an inside pirouette and is practiced facing the barre.

> Begin in fifth position with the right foot back, both hands on the barre. Use a triple-meter. Hold (a-1-&)/dégagé à la seconde en fondu with the back leg (a)/relevé retiré devant (2-&-a)/demi-plié fifth position, right foot back (3-&)/straighten (a-4-&). Repeat 4 times closing in back.

This same exercise can be done in the center with half turns, closing fifth position front and continuing in the same direction, or half-turns, alternating legs. Open the arms to second position during the dégagé à la seconde en fondu, bring them to middle fifth on the relevé, and open to second position again as the knees straighten at the end of the combination.

During the preparation en fondu, balance the weight of the body on the ball of the supporting foot. Rotate both legs equally, supporting knee over the toes and working heel in front of the foot. To turn the body, use the energy of the relevé, the rotation of the supporting leg, and the action of both the arm and the working leg. Touch the little toenail to the supporting knee at the same time the weight descends onto the ball of the supporting foot at the end of the relevé. Keep the hips square and use the rotation of the upper arm on the supporting side to resist the action of the working leg and the force of the turn. Make sure elbows are below the shoulders and the hands are below the elbows.

When the class has mastered a half-turn beginning and ending in fifth, add a preparation from fourth position. Starting from fifth position croisé devant, right

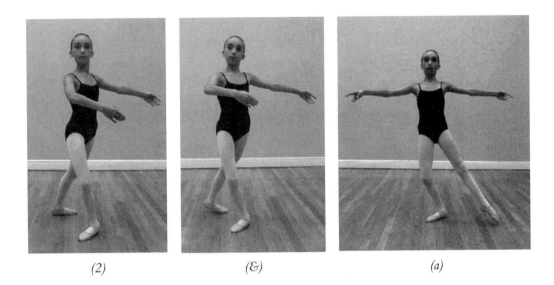

<table>
<tr><td>(2)</td><td>(&)</td><td>(a)</td></tr>
</table>

foot front, pointe tendue croisé devant (1) and lunge to fourth position (2), keeping the back knee straight.

Because the body weight is never completely over the ball of the front foot during a lunge, to prevent the back leg from pulling the body off balance as it moves to the side, a very complex shift must be made before the relevé. First lift the back heel, straightening the front knee a little (&). At this point the toes of the back foot are flexed and some weight rests on the side of the big toe. From this position push off the floor from the side of the big toe and bend the back knee to execute a développé à la seconde en fondu (a). Use the rotation of the supporting leg to turn the body to the front and the thrust of the développé to shift the weight of the body over the ball of the supporting foot in preparation for the relevé (3). Notice that the torso changes levels two times between the lunge and the pirouette.

During the lunge, place the arms in third position, right arm rounded. Open them to second position as the working leg moves à la seconde and the body shifts to face front and then bring them together in middle fifth for the turn.

> Begin in fifth position croisé devant, right foot front, arms in low fifth. Use a triple-meter. Battment tendu croisé devant, bringing the arms to middle third, right arm rounded (a-1-&-a)/lunge to fourth position (2)/straighten knee and lift heel (&)/fondu and développé a la second, taking the right arm to second position (a)/pirouette en dedans, bringing arms to middle fifth (3-&-a)/demi-plié fifth position croisé devant, left foot front, arms in middle fifth (4-&). Execute a battement tendu croisé devant with the left leg from the demi-plié, opening the right arm to second position and repeat to the other side (a-1).

Pay special attention to the placement of the supporting knee over the supporting toe. Set up the alignment during the lunge and maintain alignment through the fondu preparation and the relevé. To control the finish of the pirouette, touch the floor with both heels at the same time.

Pirouette en dehors from fourth position

Begin in fifth position with the right foot front, arms in low fifth. Use a triple-meter. Lift the arms to middle fifth on the last count of the preparation. Battement tendu à la seconde with the right leg, arms to second position (a-1-&)/demi-rond de jambe to fourth position (a-2)/demi-plié in fourth, arms middle third, right arm rounded (3-&)/deepen the plié (a)/pirouette en dehors, arms middle fifth (4-&-a)/demi-plié in fifth position, right foot back, arms in middle fifth (5-&)/straighten (a-6)/hold (7,8). Repeat to the other side. Repeat all.

Keep the weight over the ball of the supporting foot during the tendu à la seconde, the demi-rond de jambe à terre, and even in fourth position as the ball of the working foot pushes away from the floor to assist the relevé.

Prepare from a narrow fourth position so that only a slight shift will be needed to place the body on top of the supporting leg. To avoid sitting in fourth, stay on the first floor for the count and the following pulse (3-&) and then deepen the demi-plié to the basement on the second pulse (a).

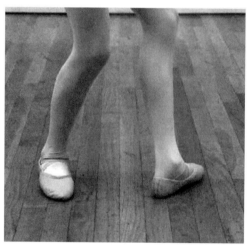

Correct

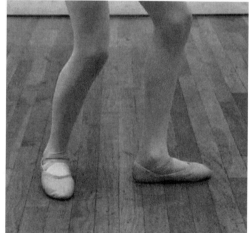

Incorrect

To power the turn, push off the floor from the balls of both feet, bring the side arm across the body to meet the other arm in middle fifth, try to open the thigh behind the shoulder, and spot the head. Remember, the working thigh is able to open and pull the body around only if the supporting side gives it something to push away from. Set up this resistance by rotating both legs equally to shape the feet in fourth position and by lifting both heels at the same time to maintain equal rotation during the relevé. Even as the thigh opens, make sure the little toenail maintains a light contact with the knee. Remember to spot the head.

The end of a pirouette is normally sustained on demi-pointe by increasing the pressure of the supporting leg into the floor at the same time the working foot pulls up a little higher under the pelvis. These two actions, however, take time to master. For the moment, encourage the dancers to catch the floor with the ball of the working foot directly in back of the supporting heel and to place both heels on the floor at the same time in fifth position demi-plié.

So many parts of the body must be coordinated to balance the body on one leg, to find enough momentum to turn one or more times on that leg, and to finish with ease and flair. What a thrill when it all comes together!

5 PETITE ALLEGRO

Preparing for petite allegro

In preparation for petite allegro, always perform a series of small jumps to warm up and to strengthen the feet. Emphasize stretching the top of the ankle and controlling the demi-plié rather than elevation.

Begin in first position with the arms in low fifth. On the first count (1) of a duple-meter, execute a demi-plié. On the following pulse (&), leave the floor just enough to point the feet. On the next count (2), return to first position demi-plié. Bend the knees and roll through the feet, touching the heels to the ground just in time to push off the floor again on the following pulse (&).

Feel as if the ceiling is one inch above your head. Feel as if the feet are kneading bread.

Once the students understand the mechanics of this type of jump, practice a series in first position. As the class progresses, apply this method of jumping to changement de pieds and, later, changement épaulement.

Changement épaulement

During changement épaulement, the direction of the body changes as well as the feet.

Execute a four-count changement, demi-plié (1)/changement (&-2)/straighten (3)hold (4)/moving from croisé, right foot front, to croisé, left foot front. As the body changes from one direction to another, keep the head erect and the focus to the front. In other words, move the body around the neck and head.

Because it is easy to overshoot fifth position croisé as the body changes direction, make a conscious effort to work within the imaginary square so that the inside of the front heel is always visible to the audience in the closing fifth.

Once the students are able to shape the correct position consistently, incline the head slightly to the front shoulder as the knees bend. Remember to keep the shoulders level as the head tilts on top of the neck.

When the class is ready, execute a series of changements épaulement.

Begin fifth position with the right foot front, croisé devant, arms in low fifth. Use a duple-meter. Demi-plié on the last count of the preparation. Changement épaulement four times (&-1)/(&-2)/(&-3)/(&-4)/straighten (5)/hold (6,7), demi-plié (8). Repeat 4 times.

Assemblé dessous

During an assemblé dessous, the working leg moves from fifth position front or back to finish under the supporting leg in fifth position back.

To lift the hips in the air, brush the ball of the working foot off the floor at the same time the ball of the supporting foot pushes off the floor. The supporting leg will open slightly as the ankle and the toes stretch. The working leg will lift about 45 degrees in response to the brush.

To keep the torso upright as it moves up and comes down, maintain a strong center. At the top of the jump rotate both legs so that the heels are in front of the feet.

> Begin in fifth position with the right foot back, arms in low fifth. Use a duple-meter. Demi-plié on the last count of the preparation. Glissade derrière (&-1)/assemblé dessus (&-2)/sousous (3)/demi-plié (4)/échappé sauté two times, using the arms (&-5,&-6)/(&-7,&-8). Repeat to the other side and then reverse the exercise.

Sissonne fermée effacé en avant

> Begin in fifth position with the right foot front, effacé devant, arms in low fifth. Use a duple-meter. Prepare the arms through middle fifth, to first arabesque, right arm front, on the second and third counts of a four-count preparation and demi-plié on the fourth count. Sissonne fermée effacé en avant 3 times (&-1)/(&-2)/(&-3)/changement to effacé devant, left foot front, changing arms to first arabesque left arm front (&-4). Repeat to the other side. Repeat all.

Spiral the upper body in opposition to the rotation of the back leg, and maintain a strong center with the ribs closed to keep the upper body from rearing back during the spring.

Execute the sissonne within the imaginary square. When moving effacé en avant, face the body so that the back heel is visible both in the starting fifth and in the final fifth.

Keep the front arm parallel to the line of the chin and look over the hand during the sissonne. Stretch the side arm back in the shoulder in opposition to the spiral of the upper body. Pull both arms with equal energy from the center of the back.

Open both legs equally to shape an inverted V. Note that the distance traveled should be equal to the height of the spring.

As vocabulary and skills increase, create combinations that can be reversed. Reversing a combination is fun and challenging for students. First discuss the meaning of the word "reverse" and then demonstrate how the process applies to an exercise the class has been practicing. Make sure that the primary combination consists of steps that can be performed clearly, easily, and skillfully. As students advance, encourage the students to figure out how to reverse a combination on their own so that problem-solving ability is developed.

Sissonne ouvert effacé en avant

Ouvert describes a sissonne that finishes open, on one leg.

> Begin in fifth positon with the right foot front, effacé devant, arms in low fifth. Use a duple-meter. Prepare the arms through middle fifth to first arabesque, right arm front, on the second and third counts of a four-count preparation and demi-plié on the fourth count. Sissonne fermée effacé en avant (&-1)/sissonne fermée effacé en avant (&-2)/sissonne ouverte effacé en avant (&-3)/pas de bourrée dessous to face effacé devant, changing arms to first arabesque left arm front (&-a)/demi-plié fifth position, left foot front (4). Repeat to the other side. Repeat all.

At the top of the sissonne ouverte shape a narrow V so that the height of the back leg is able to increase during the arabesque en fondue at the end of the jump. Look over the front hand during the sissonnes and then change the focus to the other hand during the pas de bourrée.

Assemblé devant

Assemblé devant is executed to the front with the front leg but does not travel to the front. As before, brush the working foot off the floor at the same time the supporting foot pushes off the floor to lift the hips in the air. Form an inverted V-shape in the air, lifting the working leg to 45 degrees, but this time reach toward the floor with the supporting leg to insure the vertical alignment of the torso. To control the landing, roll through the feet and lower both heels to the floor at the same time.

Begin in fifth position with the right foot front, arms in low fifth. Use a duple-meter. Prepare the arms to second position. Demi-plié (1)/assemble devant (&-2)/changement (&-3)/straighten (4). Repeat left foot front. Repeat all.

Pas coupé

Pas coupé, or cutting step, refers to the action of replacing one leg with another through fifth position in preparation for the step that follows.

Begin in fifth position with the right foot front, arms in low fifth. Use a duple-meter. Sissonne simple (&-1)/pas coupé (2)/assemblé devant (&-3)/changement (&-4). Repeat to the other side. Repeat all.

In the above combination, fold the foot into the floor through the ball of the foot as if pushing down on a coiled spring. Just before the back heel reaches the floor, begin to brush out of fifth position with the front foot. Push off the ball of the back foot and brush off the floor with the front foot on the pulse before the third count.

Increase the difficulty level by adding arm movements. Bring the arms to middle fifth on the sissonne simple, sweep them through low fifth during the coupé, and lift them to shape a V extending side from the shoulders on the ascent of the assemblé devant. Return the arms to low fifth as the feet return to fifth position demi-plié.

6 BATTERIE

Royale

Introduce royale, a beaten changement, when the class is ready.

> Begin in fifth position with the right foot front, arms in low fifth. Use a duple-meter. Demi-plié (1)/royale (&)/demi-plié (2)/straighten (3)/hold (4). Repeat left foot front. Repeat all.

The beat should feel like a high-five. Open the legs slightly as the hips lift and before coming down, bounce one leg off the other at the kissing spot. As with the soubresaut, practice the beat sitting on the floor. Use the hands to support the body, leaning back as the legs extend and lift to the front.

GRAND ALLEGRO

A grand waltz by its very nature can change a petite allegro into a grand allegro. The fullness and flow of the music alone inspires a dancer to cover as much space and jump as high as possible.

> Begin in fifth position with the right foot front, effacé devant, arms in low fifth. Carry the arms through middle fifth to first arabesque, right arm front, on the second and third counts of the preparation and demi-plié on the fourth count. Sissonne ouverte effacé en avant (&-1)/pas de bourrée dessous to demi-plié fifth position effacé devant facing left, left foot front, changing arms to first arabesque left arm high (&-a-2). Alternate to the right and left, moving downstage.

> Begin in fifth position with the right foot front, croisé devant, arms in low fifth, head inclined to the front shoulder. Sissonne tombée effacé en avant to the right (&-1)/pas de bourrée to face front (&-a)/demi-plié (2)/glissade derrière (&-3) assemblé dessus écarté devant to finish croisé devant, right foot front (&-4). Start in the upstage left corner and move diagonally downstage.

In the above combination change the direction of the body as it goes up during both the sissonne tombée and the assemble dessus écarté. Move the arms through middle fifth to second during the sissonne tombée and through second to low fifth on the pas de bourrée. During the assemblé écarté devant, move the curved arms into two straight lines extending to the side of the body, palms down. Place the arm corresponding to the working leg slightly higher than the shoulder and the other arm even with the shoulder. Direct the head and focus over the hand of the higher arm. At the finish in demi-plié fifth position croisé devant, return both arms to low fifth, head inclined to the right, eyes front.

Use the arms to assist elevation by lifting them at the same time the legs lift the body. Remember that the neck, shoulders, and arms should not reflect the effort of the jump.

8 Point Work

If your students have completed three years of serious training, taking two classes a week during the third year and attending at least one summer course, and if they are between the ages of ten and eleven, some may be ready to go en pointe sometime during the beginning of the fourth year. Understand that point readiness is a highly individual matter. In anticipation of this event, think of the last half of the third year as pre-point.

Emphasize that shoe selection is so important for their physical development, and show them how to try on new point shoes. Show them how to make shoes pliable, how to attach the ribbons and elastic to the shoes, and how to tie the ribbons. Put on your point shoes and demonstrate how a strong center, well-shaped ankles, correct balance and body alignment affect the ability to stand on the tips of the toes. Teach the class how to roll through the foot using a Theraband©—and encourage them to practice this exercise often. As they balance at the end of an exercise or execute a pirouette, a relevé, or a piqué, ask them to imagine what it might feel like to perform the same steps en pointe. Emphasize the way every aspect of the technique they have been learning will ready them for the exciting world of point work.

Part IV

Final Notes for Teachers

1 RUNNING YOUR OWN STUDIO

Running your own studio is hard work, but you do have the advantage of being your own boss and setting the standards. First, find an adequate, affordable space zoned for a ballet school. Strip malls and warehouse districts are typical choices, but make sure the area is safe and accessible to neighborhoods with families.

Once you have rented a space, install a dependable answering machine and purchase a safe floor, sturdy ballet barres, a chalkboard, a few good CDs, and a CD player, one with good sound quality and easy to use. If finances are limited, buy used items. Wait to install mirrors and construct partitions once your enrollment increases. If necessary, use a bathroom as a dressing room.

Decide on your curriculum. Are you going to offer other dance styles or only ballet? Will you need to hire other teachers or can you handle everything yourself? Who will do the billing? Who will clean the studio?

Advertise in community newspapers or distribute printed flyers by hand to businesses, especially the local dancewear distributors. Post flyers on community bulletin boards, develop your own web page, and most importantly don't forget the Yellow Pages. If you print a brochure, make sure it includes the name, address, website, and telephone number of your studio, a statement of purpose, information about tuition costs, a schedule of classes, and a yearly calendar listing holidays concurrent with those of your local school system.

When to begin training

Seven is the ideal age to begin the study of ballet. At that age children are able to concentrate on a single task for an extended period of time and have the co-ordination needed to master the basic skills of the technique. Furthermore, a child that begins her training at seven is usually able to master the ballet syllabus by the age of seventeen, the logical age to consider dancing professionally.

A pre-ballet program is an option for the younger set but only if it develops a love of movement and music, a child's imagination, and age-appropriate skills. Make sure that any instructor working with this age group is caring, creative, and knowledgeable about child development.

Registration

Collect and file pertinent information about each student including all contact numbers (home, office, and cell), addresses of parents and/or caregivers. Note the student's age, date of registration, and the number of years trained. If possible register a new student in person so that you can meet the child and show her and her parents around. Invite them to observe a class if one is in session.

Make sure parents know that their child will need proper attire by the first day. A child is usually embarrassed if she is the only one without shoes or tights. Make arrangements with your local dancewear business to stock up on the appropriate colors and sizes.

Keep monthly records of all money that comes in and goes out. Devise a logical and organized system of billing, what needs to be paid and what is owed. Keep receipts and cancelled checks in preparation for filing taxes.

Sometimes a parent might offer to provide a service for you in exchange for classes. When I first opened my studio I had one set of parents who together built my floor, installed mirrors, and later made sets and costumes for our concerts. I gave the whole family free classes for life.

If a student comes to you from another studio, reserve the right to place that student in a level appropriate to her experience and ability after observing her in a class. Parents sometimes disagree with the grade placement of their child. Help them understand the reasons behind your choice.

Studio rules

Choose rules that will help your studio run smoothly and provide your students with a structured, professional environment. Explain the reason for each rule and how the rules relate to the profession of dance.

Dress code

What kind of tights and shoes should be worn? Do you want the color of the leotard to indicate the level of the student? Are sweaters permitted on cold days, and, if so, should they be fitted? Are leg warmers or feet warmers allowed? Jewelry? What hairstyle is appropriate? Think your dress code through. It will be tested continuously. If rules are broken what will be the consequences? Do you give a warning, a time-out, call the parent?

Tardiness

Do you lock your classroom to tardy students or let them come in during the first few exercise of the barre?

Breaks

Can they drink water throughout class or only in between the barre and center floor work? What about trips to the bathroom? Can they sit down if they don't feel well? Can they get back up if they feel better?

Terms of address

Will they call you Miss Judy or Ms. Newman? Don't be too casual. Be a caring authority figure, not a buddy.

Class observation

Will it be upon request or will you have open house one day a month? This question is not applicable, of course, if you install an observation window for viewing.

Student conferences

Will you schedule conferences with parents throughout the year to discuss a child's progress or will you be available any time?

Using the telephones

Are cell phones allowed? (I hope not. This means you!)

Refunds

If the student drops out in the middle of the month, will you return any or all of the tuition?

Student safety

Who is allowed to pick up the student after class? Keep a list and make no exceptions. (Never leave a student alone. There are too many dangers lurking in the world today).

Scholarships

Will you offer scholarships, and if so, what criteria must be met?

Even if your rules and regulations are listed in your brochure, post the list as a constant reminder for parents and students.

Performing

Give beginning students a taste of performing by inviting the parents to an open house at the end of the year. Present a class and a short dance made up of the material the students have learned. Encourage them to attend a performance of the local *Nutcracker* or the yearly concert of your advanced students so they will have something to strive for.

If you do decide to use all your students in a performance at the end of the year, make sure to rehearse on the weekends or after class. While a recital might attract new students and make money, it should not take away from class time.

TEACHING TIPS 2

Learning styles

A ballet class by its very nature addresses all learning styles. The teacher communicates with words or by touch, the students watch and imitate the actions of others, they hear music that supports their movements, they sometimes teach each other, they see themselves in the mirror, and some are able to tune in to the inner workings of the body. Try to speak to all styles when you present a concept or make a correction, so that each and every student is able to learn in their own particular way. For example, if you want to remind a student to turn out the working leg during a battement tendu à la seconde, first ask her to do so. If that doesn't work, physically shape the student's leg by holding the supporting hip and gently turning the working leg in the hip. Ask her to look in the mirror or even close her eyes to feel where her heel is in relationship to her foot or if both hips are even. Ask her to watch how you do it both correctly and incorrectly. Ask her to feel how your standing leg rotates to resist the action of the working leg. Ask her to observe and assess another student as that student executes the movement.

Appealing to the imagination of any student is often a sure-fire path to comprehension. To help visualize rotation, ask a student to think of an imaginary ribbon wrapped around her leg, a candy-cane stripe starting from the inside of the upper thigh and flowing through the heel of the working foot. To shape a foot, ask her to stick her heel forward like she is sticking out her tongue. To achieve a balance between rotation and resistance, suggest that her thighs are arm wrestling and the contest is tied. Imagery usually gets a point across quickly, and because it is colorful and funny, it seemingly stays forever in the memory.

Try all the keys to find which one unlocks the door. Stand on your head if it helps a child understand. Be creative and persevere.

Assessing progress

Working with a group of students consistently allows you to evaluate the effectiveness of your teaching. Just look at your dancers. The way they work and behave lets you know if the information you are providing is being understood, if you are moving too quickly or slowly through your syllabus, if more repetition is needed, if they are excited or if they are bored. Stay open to their needs and consider it your responsibility to find ways to help them grow.

Look at all your dancers when evaluating your effectiveness, not just the talented few. Some children are so gifted technically and artistically, they improve if they show up for class. Don't take credit for them. Count yourself successful when you solve alignment problems, draw out expressive qualities, or build confidence in those not so gifted. I believe your greatest satisfaction as a teacher comes from helping a student achieve what no one imagined she could achieve.

Behavior problems

Set limits, explain the consequences, follow through, and be consistent. This system works well for most children. They may test it from time to time, but usually a gentle reminder or following through with a consequence restores order. It sounds easy enough, but sometimes a reminder and a consequence doesn't do the job. You may find a student who acts out continuously. When this happens, talk to the child privately. Express concern and disappointment. If she does better, reward her. Let her demonstrate a combination or take the roll.

If she continues to disrupt the class, arrange a conference with the parent. Try to determine the cause of the child's behavior. Does the student look forward to coming to class? Does she like to dance? Does she feel inadequate, frustrated, bored, or disliked? Is she having problems in school or at home? Try to determine if there is something you can do to help.

Sometimes, no matter what you do, there is no positive result. The worst part about this situation is the time and energy lost to the other children in the class who are making a choice to learn. If you own your own school, you are free to encourage the parent to involve the child in another activity, but if you are in a public school or work for someone else, you have no choice but to cope. Try to control your reactions to the child and stay focused on the students who need and want your attention. Put a rubber band on your wrist and give it a good snap to bring your attention around to what is positive in the class.

Professional ethics

If you have been employed by a studio for some time, you might find that you disagree with the management of the school or even the teaching styles of other instructors. If you cannot afford to leave, try to influence the status quo in a positive way by setting a good example. Keep your expectations high and let the improvement of your students make your point. If you leave, some students may follow, but never entice them to do so.

Apply the golden rule. Do not talk about students with other students and do not talk about teachers with other teachers or students. Avoid being caught in the middle of a disagreement. If someone does complain to you, encourage the student or other teacher to problem-solve by taking their complaint back to its source. Suggest polite and adult ways to communicate dissatisfaction. This is a teachable moment!

Digging out of a rut

So much is asked of a teacher, and while the rewards are great, they may not sustain you through the long haul. Burnout does happen. Here are some suggestions on how to stay fresh and keep the class lively.

Take a busman's holiday. When you have free time, observe another teacher. Watch class in another school, in another town. Attend conferences or dance festivals. Look for new ways of doing things, new ways of saying the same old things. Surprise your students with a fresh approach, a new order of exercises. Keep them on their toes!

Look for new information to share with your class. Use videos, the Internet, books, and magazines as resources.

Watch performances. Take a class on a field trip. Often local or visiting companies offer free admission to open rehearsals. These experiences will inspire both you and your students.

Mix it up in class. Use techno dance music one day for accompaniment. The pounding beat is usually perfect for most exercises. During the holidays, Christmas carols are fun, as well.

Dress up for holidays. Fool them on April 1. Take a day off to show a film or read a story. Invite a professional to share the story of her career.

Appreciate the importance of the work you do, focus on the valuable skills you develop beyond the glissade and the pirouette. Know that you are changing lives in ways you may never know.

3 FINAL NOTES

The ideal student

We all know in this post-Balanchine era that a ballet dancer has great feet, long legs, a skinny body, graceful arms, lovely hands, a swan's neck, a small head, and a beautiful face. In twenty years, I had three students who fit that description. One went on to dance professionally, one found ballet boring, and one found a boyfriend.

A child will generally exhibit a few ideal physical characteristics, and if those characteristics come together with drive, intelligence, artistry, and a healthy world-view, a dancer just might emerge. I've known teachers who invested all their energy in the gifted students and then were bitterly disappointed when those students chose a different path. I've seen teachers reject students because their bodies were less than perfect, students who, under the tutelage of someone less biased, later amazed everyone with their progress and achievements. Don't decide who should dance. Be there, give good information, encourage, stay open, and wait to be amazed.

The ideal teacher

There are so many different kinds of teachers in the world of dance. Some are charismatic. Some inspire quietly. Some are strict and some are easy-going, and they all have their fans. It is difficult to define the ideal teacher. I do believe, however, that all good teachers have a common denominator. They elicit trust. Their students know that there is a "real" person standing at the head of the class—one that knows what she's doing, one that loves what she's doing, one that desires to share what she knows and loves with each student, and one that wants the best for each student. And when students trust, they open up and learn.

Know that you cannot be all things to all students, but you can try. Be available, be present, be fair, be kind, be an advocate. Correct to build up, not to tear down. Guide by example, lead with strength and authority, and through it all, have fun and enjoy.

ABOUT THE AUTHOR

Judith Newman was raised in Miami, Florida, and began serious ballet training with Thomas Armour at the Miami Conservatory. At the age of 17, she received a Ford Foundation Scholarship to study at the School of American Ballet in New York. While taking classes there she attended Columbia University and Barry College in Miami, graduating with a BFA in English and Theatre Arts. She has performed as a soloist with the National Ballet of Washington in Washington, D.C., the Bayerische Staatsoper in Munich, Germany, and the Pennsylvania Ballet.

She began teaching in 1970, opening a studio in Oxnard, California. After returning to Miami, she taught at Fusion Dance, Momentum Dance Company, and the Miami Conservatory. In 1984, she became part of The Miami Dance Theatre School, and, together with Mariana Alvarez, directed a performing company for young dancers called Miami Dance Theatre. In 1992, she joined the faculty of the New World School of the Arts and became an Associate Professor. She is married to Ronald Newman and has a son, Cristopher, a daughter-in-law, Silvana, and two grandchildren, Carson and Nicholas.

ACKNOWLEDGEMENTS

My thanks to Thomas Armour, Ruth Weissen, Mariana Alvarez and Meghan Grupposo of the Miami Conservatory; Elizabeth Nuevo, Elise Nuevo, Daniela Schindo and Julianna Gillardo of the Artistic Dance Center; and Shelley Gefter and Silvana Newman for their knowledge and generosity. Special thanks to my husband Ronald for his love and support.

TRIBUTE

Thomas Armour was born in Tarpon Springs, Florida in 1909. He was first trained by Noelle Armour and then in Paris by the legendary Olga Preobrajenskaya. He was a principal soloist with the Ida Rubenstein Company, the Nijinska Company, the Woijikowski Company, and Leonid Massine's Ballet Russe de Monte Carlo. One of his most celebrated roles was Nijinski's "Spectre de la Rose."

After being drafted into Military Intelligence during World War II, Armour's dancing career ended. In 1949, he returned to South Florida where he founded the Miami Conservatory, now the oldest ballet school in Miami. In 1951, to provide stage experience for aspiring young dancers, he started the Miami Ballet Guild, later named the Miami Ballet, and co-founded the Southeastern Regional Ballet Association (SERBA).

Thomas Armour prepared countless young people for careers in dance and was esteemed by his community. He died on May 7, 2006, at the age of 97.